Adventure in Freedom

KENNIKAT PRESS SCHOLARLY REPRINTS

Dr. Ralph Adams Brown, Senior Editor

Series in
**AMERICAN HISTORY AND CULTURE
IN THE TWENTIETH CENTURY**
Under the General Editorial Supervision of
Dr. Donald R. McCoy
Professor of History, University of Kansas

ADVENTURE IN FREEDOM

Three Hundred Years of Jewish Life in America

by

OSCAR HANDLIN

KENNIKAT PRESS
Port Washington, N. Y./London

for Joanna

ADVENTURE IN FREEDOM

Copyright, 1954, by Oscar Handlin
Reissued in 1971 by Kennikat Press by arrangement
Library of Congress Catalog Card No: 70-137970
ISBN 0-8046-1428-8

Manufactured by Taylor Publishing Company   Dallas, Texas

KENNIKAT SERIES ON AMERICAN HISTORY AND
CULTURE IN THE TWENTIETH CENTURY

Preface

As 1954 draws to a close, the Jews of America will be celebrating with their neighbors the first landing of men of their religion in the United States. That is the occasion for this book.

Such commemorative celebrations can be rewarding. Like
other anniversaries, personal and social, they offer an occasion
for retrospective stocktaking. At these marks in time, we
pause to survey the way we have come in order the better to
look forward toward the direction in which we go. In our recollections of the past, we mingle several emotions. We think
with gladness of our survival, of the years gone by, and of the
successive crises surmounted. We think also, with gratifica-
tion, of our record of achievements: the great deeds performed, the contributions to the welfare of our fellow man,
the prosperity, recognition, and status we have attained. Such
sentiments are altogether appropriate to the occasion.

Yet we should be remiss in our duties to ourselves were we
to limit our commemoration to these thoughts. The year we
celebrate is 1654; but we cannot forget that the year in which
we celebrate is 1954. Nor can we, in the midst of our joy and
well-being, blot out from memory the tragic decade that has
just closed. Honesty demands that as we celebrate we have in
mind also the stark facts of our present situation. Jews have

vii

not recovered from the shock of the six million victims of the European catastrophe. Fifteen years of war have put an enormous burden upon American society. And the world today is locked in unremitting struggle between the forces of freedom and totalitarianism. We cannot, in rejoicing, overlook the questions this situation poses for us.

Therefore, this anniversary must be more than the occasion for gratitude and self-congratulation. It must entail also an effort at self-understanding. Toward that effort this volume is directed.

Its purpose has dictated its form. This is not a complete history of the Jews in the United States; nor is it in any sense an attempt to reckon up the contributions of the Jews to American society or culture. Worthy as these objectives may be, other hands will no doubt be turned to them this year.

This is rather an effort at interpretation, based on materials commonly known to scholars, but perhaps not so well known to the general reader at whom it is directed. For the latter, the work attempts to interpret the main lines of development in the past as they have a bearing upon the present and upon the problems of the future.

Nor is this in any sense an official volume. It has not been sponsored by any group or organization, but represents rather my individual hope that this historic occasion can also be a contribution to understanding.

In this spirit, with a full knowledge of its limitations and of the difficulties of the task, this book approaches a long and eventful history, seeking, by looking backward, some meaning for the present. By enlightening the present, it may thus aid all those who seek such meaning to shape their visions of the future.

Acknowledgments

In this work, even more than in our earlier ones, I must acknowledge the devoted collaboration of my wife, Mary Flug Handlin, who shared with me all the trials of composition. Without her unfailing support this would not be the book it is. I have profited also from the counsel and assistance of Samuel J. Hurwitz of Brooklyn College, of Barbara M. Solomon, of Esther Berger, and of Rabbi Isidore S. Meyer. Some of the material incorporated in this volume appeared earlier in *Commentary*, in the *American Jewish Historical Society Publications*, and in *Freedom Pamphlets*. I am grateful to the editors of those journals for valuable assistance, and to Dr. Jacob R. Marcus of the American Jewish Archives and Morris Fine of the Library of Jewish Information. The illustrations have graciously been supplied by the institutions and individuals acknowledged in the captions. The manuscript was prepared with skill and dispatch by Nancy D. Hibbard.

Contents

xi

List of Illustrations

Adventure in Freedom

CHAPTER ONE

The Jews of Colonial America

In its brief history, the struggling outpost of the Dutch West India Company on the Hudson had already seen many a curious sight. None was more curious, however, than the spectacle that greeted observers one day early in September, 1654. Beating its way up the Bay had come the tiny bark, *St. Charles*. As the vessel drifted wearily to anchor at the foot of the island, its passengers could be seen eagerly waiting to touch land. When at last they descended, it was apparent that among them were twenty-three Jews.

Such folk were indeed a rarity in this corner of the New World. Through the tiny settlements that dotted the Atlantic Coast of North America, an occasional individual of that religion may have drifted without leaving a trace of his presence in the record. But this was the first group to make its way to the lands that ultimately became the United States; and they established the first organized Jewish community in that region.

There was dramatic appropriateness to the tricks of fortune that assigned the role of founders to such men as these. Like the millions of Jews who would follow in the next three centuries, the passengers of the *St. Charles* reached their destination at the end of a series of wanderings in search of a home.

The new arrivals had come a long way. In the first instance,

3

the road they had followed reached back to Brazil. Briefly, in that lush corner of South America, the twists of international colonial rivalry had made a place for the Jews. Until 1630, the territory had been a possession of the Portuguese who, like the Spaniards, had refused to permit heretics or unbelievers to enter their overseas dominions. Only for a single year, in 1624, while Holland held Bahia had the Israelites been allowed to settle there openly. Then in 1630, Recife had fallen to the Dutch, more tolerant and willing to encourage the settlement of the Jews in their newly gained possession. While the Netherlanders remained in control, the Jews prospered; a thriving community sprang into being in Recife and flourished for a quarter-century. Yet here, too, hopes of a permanent home were doomed to disappointment. With the reconquest of Recife by the Portuguese in 1654, it was no longer safe for Jews to remain. In flight from the new Brazilian order, the passengers of the *St. Charles* had come to New Amsterdam.

To Brazil, their road had led across the Atlantic from the Netherlands. In the Dutch provinces, the Jews had discovered a refuge. That thriving country, self-confident in the aftermath of its successful struggle for liberation against Spain, was well on the way to commercial and financial primacy in the Western world. There Jews were free to live in the seventeenth century, free to create healthy communities and to participate in the economic and cultural life of the growing nation. Few in numbers, they had nevertheless already established themselves in trade and industry.

The Jews, to whom Holland offered a resting place, had come mostly from Spain and Portugal. Amsterdam had now become a magnet that drew Jews also from Germany and the east. But the roots of the passengers on the *St. Charles* reached back to the Iberian Peninsula; they continued for some time to refer to themselves as "of the Portuguese nation." Landing on Manhattan, they were completing the last stage of the dissolution of the Sephardic culture of medieval Spain.

For centuries, the Jews of the Peninsula had displayed astonishing vigor. In a long golden age, they had given to Spain economic and political leadership and to Europe and the world, men of learning and of science. With the growth of centralized royal authority and the consolidation of a national state in the fifteenth century, the world of Spanish Jewry had begun to dissolve. Restrictive measures pressed them to abandon their ancestral faith. Suspicion drove the Inquisition to violently repressive measures. Finally, by an ironic—almost providential —coincidence, in the very year of Columbus's discovery of America, the Jews of Spain were expelled. A royal edict compelled them to leave unless they adopted Christianity.

Some chose as the lesser evil the appearance of conversion and adopted the outward forms of Christianity, although many Marranos remained secret adherents of Judaism. Time and again some such person, arriving at a sanctuary where his hidden faith was not a menace, revealed himself openly a Jew.

In the face of the decree of expulsion, some Jews still refused to yield, even outwardly, and preferred to leave Spain altogether. In the next century and a half they drifted about the face of Europe. They wandered eastward to Italy and to Turkey. They moved northward, establishing themselves in the Netherlands, at Hamburg, around the Baltic, and later in England. Often men of wealth, experienced in business or possessors of professional skills, they contributed substantially to the civilizations to which they came.

Yet, they remained still strangers, with their grandiloquent Spanish names, seeking to reconstruct the forms of a life that had long since vanished. And a goodly number never managed to attain economic security, but were driven to still newer places in the quest for a home and for opportunity. From this ultimate source the first trickle had flowed to the New World in 1654.

The score of them landed at New Amsterdam and, unable to pay for their passage, were at once clapped into jail. The testy Governor Stuyvesant saw no need of such newcomers and required them "in a friendly way to depart." But the Dutch West India Company, influenced by its Jewish stockholders, was more liberal and granted the strangers the rights of settlers "provided the poor among them" be no burden, "but be supported by their own nation." They stayed, and in time found themselves a community. In time too, scattered handfuls of others like themselves added to their numbers. By the end of the century, they totaled perhaps a hundred.

After 1700 other groups of immigrants joined them, some still continuing the Sephardic migration, some drawn from other parts of Europe. By the middle of the eighteenth century there were some three hundred Jews in the City of New York.

Meanwhile, other lesser communities had come into being in Newport, in Philadelphia, and in Charleston. Little sprinklings of Jews were also scattered along the coast from Massachusetts south to Georgia. In all, perhaps two thousand of these people lived in the colonies that were to revolt in 1776. From these meager antecedents sprang the Jewish community that would, three centuries later, be the largest and most influential in the world. The meaning of their migration lay not in the numbers actually involved, but in the situation they prepared for the millions who would follow later.

It was not likely, as they stepped ashore at New Amsterdam, that the passengers of the *St. Charles* imagined this would be any more permanent a home for them than the other ends of the earth they had already touched. This was the post of a trading company, not far different from others like it in the Caribbean and in South America or, for that matter, in Africa and Asia—a fortified place for the exchange of manufactured goods and native products.

To the south and north were similar plantations. On the Delaware River, the Swedes had for a time nurtured a little colony until the more powerful Dutch swallowed it up. In New England, British subjects had by now put on a sure footing the settlements in Massachusetts, New Hampshire, Rhode Island, Plymouth, and Connecticut; and around Chesapeake Bay they were firmly established in Virginia and Maryland. Within the decade, the whole territory would be English, for the Hollanders were doomed to see New England become Charles II's royal province of New York. Before long there would be added the new British colonies of Georgia and the Carolinas, Pennsylvania and the Jerseys.

However, not the changes of jurisdiction or sovereignty, but rather the transformation of its population, gave an exceptional character to this part of America. The early trading companies had discovered that they could not here, as in Mexico and India, simply deal with natives for the natural wealth of the place. Here there were neither gold, nor jewels, nor exotic tropical crops, nor many Indians to exploit. What wealth this country boasted—tobacco, fish, furs—called for hands to draw it forth; and these hands could be supplied only by immigrants attracted to permanent residence.

Natural conditions in these colonies therefore encouraged a large and growing population that had decisively cut itself off from its antecedents, resolved to build a new life in the New World. Some came voluntarily out of the ambition to become landowners, others were brought over as indentured servants or kidnapped and captured without their consent. Still others migrated, as did the Puritans, the Quakers, and the German Pietistic sects, out of the desire to construct new kinds of societies in the open spaces of America. Mostly such people turned to agriculture, and spread settlement inward toward the wilderness. By 1770 farmers were the bulk of the two and a quarter million residents of the colonies.

Yet colonial farming was always dependent upon trade. Whether the product was one of the tropical staples—tobacco, rice, indigo—or whether it came from the diversified farms that produced wheat, meat, and fish, farming could yield a return only through the services of the merchants who found overseas markets. The trading communities of the cities remained, as they had been at the start, essential to the prosperity of the settlements. And given the rapid growth of the colonies, there was room for all manner of outsiders to find places in commerce.

By the nature of their own background and of the situation they discovered in America, the colonial Jews were quick to take advantage of the opportunities of trade. Although a few wandered into the back country, or settled elsewhere upon the land, the bulk of the Jews lived in the largest cities and were concerned with commerce. Experience, literacy, and family connections throughout the world, more than compensated for lack of initial capital.

Three illustrations clearly display the course of this development. Among the great merchants of Newport was Aaron Lopez. In 1752 he had come over from Lisbon, a Marrano, no doubt informed by his half-brother, already there, of the opportunities presented by the rising capital of Rhode Island. By dint of shrewd calculation and venturesome enterprise, he accumulated a moderate fortune, came to own his own ships, and managed a network of trading operations that extended along the whole Atlantic Coast and to the West Indies. Lopez's interests drew him also into industry: he was quick to see the advantages in the manufacture of spermaceti candles and, with a group of other merchants, devised the first American trust in 1761. By the time he had his portrait painted, he was not much different from any other colonial worthy; beneath his powdered wig, he looks placidly forth, a twinkle in his eyes and the hint of a smile enlivening his smooth-shaven face.

Farther south, in New York, were the headquarters of the Franks family. The family fortune had been established early in the eighteenth century by Moses Levy, who came to the new city in 1702. His daughter Abigail married a young newcomer from England, Jacob Franks. Between 1730 and 1770 the family established an extensive shipping business that reached both to the continent of Europe and to the West Indies. During the intermittent wars between the French and

English, the Franks were official purveyors to the Crown, and no doubt used that position to support their own economic affairs. By 1770 they had important branch offices in several American cities as well as in London and the West Indies, and maintained a constant correspondence that permitted them to take advantage of every fluctuation in the course of trade.

The career of Moses Lindo, for a time of Charleston, South Carolina, was somewhat different. He brought to that seaport not only unusual commercial abilities but also the technical skill that was the basis for production of one of the colonies' most important crops. Born in England, Lindo had been educated in London and by apprenticeship had become an expert in the use of dyes.

In 1748 the British Government had offered a bounty to encourage in the colonies the production of indigo, a plant from which was derived the royal-blue dye so highly valued in the growing textile industry. In South Carolina, its cultivation proceeded very slowly in the next few years, hampered by the inability to establish a proper grading and marketing system. Lindo came to Charleston in 1756 charged with the mission to contract for a large part of the crop on behalf of English dyers. In the next few years he created the channels by which that product was enabled to flow freely back to the dyeing houses of London. Lindo became the official surveyor, or inspector, with the power to establish grades and to inspect all indigo destined for export. His skill and energy proved highly advantageous to the colony as a whole as well as to himself.

Such merchants as Lopez, Franks, and Lindo set the tone for the life of colonial Jews, for they were in control of Jewish communal affairs. Certainly their ideas and interests shaped the pattern of development through the whole period.

Whether the merchants constituted an actual numerical majority of American Jews is difficult to tell. Humbler folk were, of course, less likely to attract public notice or to leave behind personal documents. Now and then there do appear, in the records of the seventeenth and eighteenth centuries, some Jews who "earn their living by manual labor." Occasionally an artisan emerges from the obscurity to which history confines little people, and a butcher or a baker proves to have been Jewish. Better known were the skilled handicraftsmen, some of whom were fabricators of the precious metals. Thus Levy Simons, embroiderer, informed New Yorkers in an advertisement that he worked in gold and silver, as well as in silk, worsted, and lace; and Myer Myers for a time was president of the Silversmith's Society of New York. Less numerous still were professional men. In Maryland, a Dr. Lombroso makes himself known in court proceedings; Samuel Nuñez practices in Georgia; and a handful of physicians elsewhere ply their craft. But the numbers are few, and it is likely that some of these also engaged in trade. In any event, all these people deferred to the merchants who took the lead in communities dominated by mercantile interests.

Life in America thus seemed to the Jews largely an extension of the life they had long led in the Old World. They had simply wandered to another corner of the globe where they expected, as in earlier migrations, to find a temporary resting place. That this would be any more home to them than Brazil or Holland or Spain was beyond their anticipations. As long as they were tolerated, they would make themselves useful in trade and otherwise.

A tiny group in a distant land, they expected to cling together, to aid one another, and to shape a common life in the New World as in the Old. But they envisioned in America no decisive break between past and present.

For centuries in their European past, the Jews had existed as an enclave within a larger society. All about them was an active and variegated life, in which other men tilled the soil or exercised artisan trades, were members of villages or guilds, and were communicants of an established church. From all those activities the Jews had been cut off. They had survived instead through confinement to a ghetto, the walls of which were restrictive whether they were built of stone or of binding laws and customs.

Within the European ghetto the members of the community necessarily hung together. It was not here a matter of choice, of belonging or not belonging; all Jews were identified as such by their birth and by the very conditions of their life in this society. In the face of the hostile outer world, all within the walls felt responsible for one another's actions. They accepted and supported a variety of organizations for control, aid, and service.

The European community was thus tightly knit. It exercised great power over its members, and its influence extended to every aspect of existence in the ghetto. As the *Kahal*, or congregation, it conducted religious worship; but it also administered law and the educational, charitable, and social systems. Nor did it hesitate to regulate the private lives of those it governed. The congregation had power to tax its members, and behind its every pronouncement were the weightiest sanctions: excommunication, social ostracism, and in some times and places, the authority of the civil government. The self-perpetuating officers, generally the wealthy, held substantial power.

The Jews of the New World attempted, as a matter of course, to reestablish such communities. They expected in their new places of sojourn to live together, to worship together, and to aid one another as they always had. But slow and uncertain growth delayed them; it took some forty years before the Jews were firmly enough settled in New York to found their first congregation. In the eighteenth century, other Jewish communities in other cities followed in establishing the traditional forms and organizations as soon as they were large enough. But the effort was only partially and temporarily successful. Time and again the congregations were driven to compromise and expediency. By 1770 they had decisively entered upon a process of change that would make their institutions altogether different from those of Europe.

In part, the disruption of the old communal life was due to the difficulties of the new environment. Nothing was available, nothing could be taken for granted. Not the buildings or the cemeteries, not the holy books or the teachers to interpret them, not the scrolls of Law or the ceremonial objects appropriate to festivals, not even the traditional lunar calendar. It required effort and determination to observe the complex requirements of tradition. Late in the eighteenth century, Aaron Lopez had to send from Newport to New York for a man competent to circumcise his son. Not many could afford to do the same, or to meet the myriad practical obligations of the religion.

Furthermore, among these people few were learned in the Law. Until well into the nineteenth century, there was not a single rabbi in the United States, and the laymen were rarely able to deal with the intricacies of the Law under these conditions. Occasionally they would write back for advice to the scholars of London or Amsterdam. What degrees of consanguinity made marriages invalid? What was the formula for divorce, the procedure for the reception of proselytes? The answers were slow in coming, or unclear, or simply not relevant. Most often, it seemed preferable to these practical businessmen to deal with each problem pragmatically as it arose, to settle questions in accord with the necessities of the situation.

And the necessities of the situation in America invariably thrust the community toward change. The social environment of Europe had receded in the transatlantic crossing; and that of the New World called for altogether new forms of social organization. For one thing, the defensive stance against outsiders relaxed. After the initial unpleasantness with old Governor Stuyvesant, the Jews found themselves welcome and quickly made at home. Everywhere the logic of empty space was clear. As the Jews of Amsterdam pointed out to the West India Company, "Yonder land is extensive and spacious," and the more loyal people occupied it, the more the colony would profit in taxes and trade. Many types of newcomers were encouraged to share in the tasks of settlement; among the many varieties of strangers, the Jews were no longer exceptional; everyone was to some extent different.

In some places they were actually treated with exceptional favor. In New England, for instance, they were very highly regarded as a group. The influence of the Old Testament and the popularity of Hebrew culture gave the Puritans a strong leaning toward the Jews. The lads whose studies at Harvard included Hebrew grew up to respect the people whose language it had been.

In addition, the Puritans assigned to the Jews a critical role in the drama of salvation. The Puritans were convinced that the second coming and the final judgment of the world were imminent; that conviction had animated their migration to the New World. They knew by the articles of their faith that conversion of the Jews would precede and would herald these providential events. In anticipation, it was certainly necessary to cherish these folk and to encourage their conversion. The Jews were a mystery, living evidence of the truth of the divine revelations, and destined to endure as such until the millennium.

Puritan friendship was demonstrated as early as the seventeenth century. In 1670 a certain Jacob Lucena found himself in difficulty in Hartford. Arrested for loose and indecent behavior, he had been sentenced to prison. When the authorities ascertained his religious affiliation, they determined to show him what "favor" they could, "considering he is a Jew"; they commuted his sentence to a fine, and ultimately spared him even that.

A century later, similar favors were shown to worthier objects. Judah Monis, in Cambridge, had had his Hebrew grammar published, and was appointed to teach at Harvard, where he became the recipient of an honorary degree. In Newport, meanwhile, the minister, Ezra Stiles, had established a warm friendship with various Jews. Indeed, during the Revolution, the serious suggestion was heard that Hebrew replace English as the official American language.

These favorable, receptive attitudes were new and unexpected; they permitted the Jews to draw close to other Americans. Occasional intermarriages were evidence that the social distance between the Jews and their fellow citizens was narrowing. More important was the growing similarity in style of life and attitudes. Like the other merchants of Newport, the Harts and Polocks had their own social club; and the synagogue of that town, the loveliest monument of early American Jewry, took the outward form of Georgian architecture that its designer, Peter Harrison, also gave to King's Chapel and Christ Church.

The result was an unprecedented institutional situation. In three vital respects the Jews discovered that altered circumstances made it difficult to maintain the community on this side of the Atlantic as it had been on the other. In America, they discovered, they were rapidly becoming the religious equals of other citizens. The contrast with the position as it still existed in Europe grew increasingly startling. In every part of the Old World, the Jews were set off as a separate, inferior, religious minority. From some countries, as from Spain, they were excluded altogether. Elsewhere, as in France, they were permitted to live a recognized, though covert, existence, without rights and completely subject to the whims of the monarch. In England, where in the mid-eighteenth century their position was at its best, they were allowed to lead a relatively stable existence, though subject to numerous discriminations. For all these Jews, tolerance was as yet a distant, ideal goal; at most, they hoped simply for the opportunity to lead their own religious life openly, without subjection to disabilities or discrimination. Nowhere was there the least expectation that their faith might ever be put on the same or on an equal footing with that established and supported by the government.

American practice, at the start, had been similar to that in Europe. In each colony an established church had been created by law, and dissent discouraged or stamped out. But practical conditions militated against the continuance of that order. The idea of establishment ran counter to the developing actuality: the diversity of the American population left no group a clear-cut majority throughout the continent; nor was any group everywhere a clear-cut inferior minority. The Puritan Congregationalists dominant in New England were elsewhere cast in the role of dissenters. The Quakers, once persecuted in Boston, now were in control in Pennsylvania. Catholics were only a tiny handful, although the proprietor of Maryland was himself a communicant of that Church. Through the interior were scattered Presbyterians and Baptists, members of the Dutch Reformed Church and German sectarians. This profusion of faiths made the very concept of establishment anachronistic, although the letter of the law lagged behind actual practice. By a succession of easy steps, Judaism came to be viewed as simply one other among numerous forms of belief and worship.

This new attitude began to evolve early. In 1649 Lord Baltimore, the proprietor of Maryland, anxious to make it possible for his fellow Catholics to live in the province, recognized that under any circumstances they would still be a minority subject to the Church of England. To give them what protection he could, he extended freedom of worship to all believers in the doctrine of the Trinity. Clearly he intended this as a liberalizing measure; yet that Jews or Unitarians might be left free to worship as they pleased occurred to no one. Some ten years later there appeared on the scene Dr. Jacob Lombroso, announcing he was a Jew and denying the divinity of Christ. The law was plain, and under it the doctor was accused of blasphemy and brought to trial. Here he openly refused to retract the offensive statements. Nevertheless the court was unwilling to condemn him to the punishment the law prescribed. The case was put off and the prosecution never resumed. Lombroso lived on, a man of substance, and the law fell into disuse, remaining unheeded on the statute books.

Elsewhere it was the same story. Religious freedom came rapidly and easily even without changes in the law. In 1685 the Jews of New York requested the privilege of maintaining public worship. After some scratching of learned legal heads, they were told the law forbade it. A few years later, they had built their synagogue, leaving the law to take care of its own adjustment. Indeed, in 1711 New York's Jews were so secure in their own rights that they could be the benefactors of others; seven of them that year contributed to the fund for building Trinity Church.

By 1770, although some legal disabilities remained on the statute books, and although an established church still existed in some colonies, actual practice had far outrun those formal limitations. In effect, the Jews had attained complete religious freedom. The equality for which the Jews of Europe did not

A view of New Amsterdam in 1667, thirteen years after the first Jews to settle in America landed there in the St. Charles, a ship similar to that in the foreground.

The Mill Street Synagogue (left) erected in New York in 1730. . . . This Newport synagogue, designed by Peter Harrison in 1763, is a splendid example of the finest colonial architecture and the loveliest monument to early American Jewry existing today. (Courtesy of Kerschner, Newport, R.I.)

dare to dream had become a reality in America; and it would take only separation from Great Britain to confirm it in law as well.

Attainment of civic equality was more complete still. In Europe many privileges were withheld from Jews. Entrance to some professions was sharply restricted; education in the universities was denied to them; and they were excluded from the practice of many trades, either by the municipal corporations or by the legally constituted guilds. A multitude of other restrictions also hedged them about. In some places, they could not contract marriages without the consent of the government.

The American colonies, on the other hand, were not bound by the ideal of a stratified, orderly life, with men assigned their places by law. Guilds did not exist in the European form, and in time trade everywhere in the colonies became free. The first comers to Manhattan had run headlong into Stuyvesant's prejudices. But successively they acquired the privileges of engaging in wholesaling, of building houses, of being rid of discriminatory taxes, of enjoying general burgher rights, and of entering into the retail and artisan trades.

In the eighteenth century the halls of learning that would remain closed to Jews for another century in England, were opened to them in America. By 1770 a number of Jewish boys had already passed through college, and in that year, the College of Rhode Island (later Brown University) announced that it would never restrict admission on the basis of religion. What had been unattainable privileges in the Old World had become a matter of course in the New. On the eve of the

Revolution, the Jews of the country had acquired what they enjoyed nowhere in Europe, complete civic equality.

Most startling of all was the acquisition of political privilege. Nowhere in Europe did Jews participate in the control of government. Not only were the states of the Old World monarchies of aristocracies with power confined in the hands of a few, but the Jews as a group were cut off from all political activity by explicit restrictions. Much later, in the nineteenth century, even the wealth of a Rothschild would not permit a Jew to take the seat in the House of Commons to which he had been elected.

Yet in America the Jews promptly secured the full political rights of citizens. In New Amsterdam, the Dutch settlers had been unwilling to be "fellow-soldiers" with Jews; such, after all, had not been the practice in Holland. But the determined protest of Asher Levy in 1655 earned him the right to stand guard like others. Early the Jews were allowed to vote and to hold elective office; in 1718 two were chosen constables in New York. In the seventeenth century as individuals they received the rights of denizens; and after 1740 an act of parliament permitted them to be freely naturalized. By the time of the Revolution, the Jews shared without question the political privileges of other Americans.

A dramatic demonstration of political equality came in 1774. As the nation moved toward revolution, an election in South Carolina produced an unprecedented situation. Among those chosen members of the provincial congress that year was Francis Salvador, a Jewish planter born in England. His selection by a constituency in which there could have been but few Jews demonstrated the extent to which Americans had become willing to commit political power to these people. Salvador would himself die fighting in the Revolution. But there was enduring significance to the position he briefly held.

Therein lay the true importance of their colonial experience. In their long history, the Jews had elsewhere reached a state of material well-being equal to that they enjoyed in the American colonies. Elsewhere, they had boasted of greater cultural achievements. But nowhere in their past was there precedent for the total equality extended to them in the American colonies. Now they were to be tested as never before by the privileges and responsibilities of freedom.

That very freedom and equality put a strain on the old communal institutions. The new conditions raised questions, pregnant with meaning. Here no man was a Jew because he had to be; here no one was subject to any restraints except those to which he voluntarily submitted. The congregation could not count on holding its members by a discipline imparted from without, but only by playing a meaningful part in their lives. To these new conditions the growing community would adjust itself in the decades after 1770, as the Revolution and independence completed the process begun in the American colonial past.

CHAPTER TWO

The Life of the Young Republic

For more than a half-century after 1770 the American people were preoccupied with the problems of independence. Through the first ten years of that period, they were involved in the Revolution that cut them apart from the British Empire; and in the decades that followed they concerned themselves in a multitude of ways with the necessity of completing the process by which they became a nation. In this momentous span of years the forces took form that were later to shape American culture, society, economics, and politics. Every aspect of these changes touched the lives of the Jews of the United States.

Three strands were woven into the Revolution: the concrete economic grievances of the colonists against the imperial system within which they were bound; the sense of nationality of a rising people resentful of lack of recognition; and certain ideal conceptions of freedom and right denied or violated by the existing political order. On each of these counts, Jews were, with few exceptions, drawn into the struggle just like other Americans.

The Jews who were merchants shared the resentment of most men in trade at the restrictions of the navigation acts and the severity of the British customs officials. A few, like some of their neighbors, ultimately lost heart, or for some other reason became loyalists. But the great majority were signers of the nonimportation agreements and took the successive steps after 1763 that led toward active resistance.

As much as anyone in the colonies, Jews felt the attractiveness of the emerging conception of nationality. They liked also to think of themselves as distinctive, as evolving in a way apart from that of Europeans. On this continent, they thought, there had appeared a new man, descended from all the races of the Old World, but unlike any of them, and destined in the future to assume a newer, better form. The Jews had had no sense of belonging to nations to whose past they were alien; but here, in a nation that was all future and no past, they could be one in sentiment with every other citizen. Nor were loyalties to Britain likely to hold them back in any respect.

Finally, the revolutionary ideals of equality and freedom promised to consolidate the gains in status they had already made in the New World. The self-evident truths that all men were created equal and were equally endowed with certain natural rights opened up the roseate vista of total legal and social recognition of the advances the Jews were already making in practice.

Therefore, the Revolution summoned forth the best energies of American Jews. They expended devotion and effort far beyond their duty, and far more than their numbers required; and they contributed substantially to the winning of American independence.

Three men illustrate in their lives the many services rendered the revolutionary cause.

In Newport, Aaron Lopez, now grown wealthy and rich

in the respect of his neighbors, understood the consequences of the decisive events as they unfolded. He did not flinch from the course his conscience pointed, when the city fell into the hands of the British soldiers. To remain meant an opportunity to retain his property, but also the obligation to collaborate with his country's oppressors. To flee, on the other hand, entailed the risk of losing all that years of effort had brought him.

Lopez did not hesitate. With his family he escaped northward and settled in the little Massachusetts town of Leicester. There he remained through the war, without bitterness, steadfast in his faith in the infant republic, and pleased with his sacrifice on its behalf. This "amiable, benevolent" gentleman died in 1781—"without a single enemy & the most universally beloved . . . of any man I ever knew," wrote the Rev. Ezra Stiles. "His beneficence to his family & connexions, to his nation, & to all the world is," the future president of Yale added, almost "without a parallel."

In Philadelphia in 1778 a young man not long since an immigrant from Poland sought work in the cause. Haym Salomon had come to New York in 1775, in quest of a fortune through trade. He had done moderately well in commerce when the outbreak of war threw his affairs into disorder. From the start, he was a patriot. When the British took the city, he worked secretly against them, aiding those they had captured to escape. Finally he rejected an opportunity for profitable collaboration and ran off to Philadelphia to enlist in the struggle for independence.

At the seat of the Continental Congress, he found his opportunity for a unique kind of service which capitalized on his special talents. Heavy wartime expenses made the government desperate for funds, yet neither the machinery of enforcement nor public confidence were strong enough to yield it much through taxation. The war could be financed only through loans or through printing paper money. Both expedients threw the currency into chaos. The new states and the Continental Congress each printed its own bills which, unsupported, began a dizzy downward drop in value. As the bewildering bits of paper multiplied, men scarcely knew their worth or their prospect for redemption.

The loans were also perplexing. Mostly they came from abroad and in good part the proceeds had to be remitted to France and Holland for supplies. The medium of these operations was the Bill of Exchange; and quickly these, too, became common and of uncertain value in Philadelphia. Salomon became a broker, trading in notes and paper of every kind. Before long he was the most expert in the city and began to act on behalf of the government. He became a close associate of Robert Morris, the superintendent of finance, and was of immense assistance in the complicated negotiations that financed the war.

Salomon was thus a businessman, trading in bills from which he hoped to profit. What distinguished him was not the altruism of his character, but rather the basis of that expectation for profit. His hopes of gain rested upon the faith that the struggle for independence would be successful; and the confidence with which he supported the government in the crisis was more precious than gold. Others occasionally held back and hesitated, but this American, though less than a decade in the country, had never a doubt. More than one member of the Continental Congress, in addition, found it possible to remain in Philadelphia through credit extended without charge by Salomon.

Fighting in Georgia was Benjamin Nones, a native of Bourdeaux, France. This young man had still been in Europe when the Revolution broke out. He was one of several European Jews, fired with enthusiasm, who came across to participate in a battle that they knew was theirs. He served bravely in the Continental Army, distinguishing himself in the siege of Savannah and the battle of Camden.

These men were not alone. Like Lopez, most of the Congregation Shearith Israel of New York left the city rather than cooperate with the British. Like Salomon, Isaac Franks and Leon Moses helped finance the war. And like Nones, Mordecai Sheftall and Francis Salvador bore arms for the new nation. All acted for the sake of principles worth fighting for. And the end of the war brought them not only the satisfaction of victory but also the exhilarating sense of having established the validity of those principles. "An intier new scene will open it self," wrote Mordecai Sheftall in 1783, when he learned the war had ended, "and we have the world to begin againe."

The spirit that had animated the Revolution continued for many years to influence the new nation. Although this had been a national struggle, the men of 1776 had not construed nationality in any narrow sense. Their cause, they had said, was the cause of all mankind. And because Europeans had believed that was so, men like Nones, together with Lafayette, Pulaski, DeKalb, Koscuisko, and others, had thrown in their lot with the Americans.

When, therefore, men turned their thoughts to the means of consolidating the gains of the Revolution, they had no desire to limit those gains to residents already settled in the land. On the contrary, following the Revolution for a long time thereafter, Americans intended to welcome any newcomers who chose to come, confident that anyone, by coming, could transform himself into an American.

Actually, not many immigrants made the crossing between 1790 and 1815. For a quarter-century the wars touched off by the French Revolution disrupted all the routes of trade, made travel hazardous, and reduced international movements to a trickle. Among those who did come through, there continued to be a scattering of Jews, enough to increase their numbers in the United States to perhaps five thousand by 1820 as compared with the total population that year of almost ten million.

In the relative stability of these years, while connections with Europe were at their weakest, Americans strove to eliminate residual relics of the past, to bring their institutions into conformity with the ideals for which they had fought. Among the matters that attracted their attention was the desirability of extending the conception of religious equality by adjusting law to practice and by entirely separating church from state.

Vestiges of establishment persisted in some places in the form of government support for churches or for religious education. Elsewhere the statute books still held laws prescribing a religious oath as a prerequisite for office-holding. But a decisive contest in Virginia in 1776 had already disestablished the Anglican Church. And Jefferson and Madison in 1785 firmly set forth the principles of religious equality as they induced the state, in a Bill for Establishing Religious Freedom, to proclaim that *"the opinions of men are not the object of*

civil government, nor under its jurisdiction." New York and
Pennsylvania followed shortly thereafter. And the Federal
Constitution, in the provision against test oaths and in the
first amendment, built a solid wall of separation between
church and state. In a parade celebrating the ratification, in
1789, a contemporary saw "the clergy of different denominations with the rabbi of the Jews walking arm in arm." (The
title "rabbi" was then, as often, given the "minister" or cantor
of the congregation.)

In a few states the older provisions lingered, but without
the capacity to resist any sustained attack. They were so dis-
cordant with the beliefs to which all Americans subscribed,
that they disappeared as soon as their invidious character was
challenged. In 1809 North Carolina abolished the discriminatory clause in its constitution, and seventeen years later Maryland did the same. By then some anachronistic terminology
still remained on the statute books of a few states, but religious
distinctions were nowhere recognized in the United States.

When Washington took office as first president, the principle was expressed in words of noble clarity in his exchange
of correspondence with the Jews of Newport. On behalf of
the congregation, Moses Seixas had communicated to Washington the joy of the Jews, as free citizens, to "behold a government which to bigotry gives no sanction, to persecution
no assistance, but generously" affords "to ALL liberty of conscience and immunities of citizenship—deeming everyone, of
whatever nation, or language, equal parts in the great govern-
mental machine." In response, the President had pointed out,
"It is now no more that toleration is spoken of, as if it was by
the indulgence of one class of people that another enjoyed the

exercise of their inherent natural rights. For happily the Government of the United States . . . requires only that they who live under its protection should demean themselves as good citizens . . . while every one shall sit in safety under his own vine and fig-tree, and there shall be none to make him afraid."

Thereafter, the extension of civic and political rights was a general problem, not one that affected Jews alone; whatever restrictions remained were in terms of property or other social, rather than religious, qualifications. However, all such limitations on suffrage and office-holding were shortly to disappear or to be rendered invalid; and with them vanished the last traces of legal privilege in the economic, political, and social life of the nation. In this general diffusion of democracy, Jews benefited together with other Americans. In 1820, at the consecration of the synagogue in Savannah, Dr. Jacob De La Motta could indeed exclaim, "On what spot in this habitable Globe does an Israelite enjoy more blessings, more privileges?"

For the Jews of America, therefore, the forty years after 1780 were a period of relative calm and of growing stability. Their numbers mounted, but not radically. Increasingly they were native-born, and the children and grandchildren of native-born Americans. They were at home in America and well adjusted to its life.

As earlier, the merchants set the predominant tone of the group. Some of the great families of the past had fallen upon poorer times. Newport, in particular, never recovered from the disasters of the Revolution, and its Jews never regained their former prosperity. But in other places the restoration of trade was quick and efficacious. Population pushed steadily across the mountains, and the pulse of internal exchange quickened. Fortunate as a neutral while other powers were at war, the United States raised the volume of its overseas commerce ever higher; ships destined for every port in the world crowded the wharves of such old cities as New York and Philadelphia, of such new ones as Baltimore and New Orleans.

In Philadelphia, the Gratz family had established itself early in the eighteenth century and by the 1770s had become interested in Western lands. They then dispatched George Croghan into the Ohio country to survey desirable tracts. From their headquarters in Philadelphia, members of the family acquired substantial interests in the fur trade and in land. Farther south, Jacob Cohen and Isaiah Isaacs became similarly active; the record of their dealings with Daniel Boone still survives, sprinkled with Yiddish phrases. Such enterprising men had their own profit in view as they thought of the West; but they nevertheless played a significant role in the great thrust of settlement after the war. The speculator opened up the virgin wilderness by believing in its potentialities, by making information available, by subdividing plots, and by directing to the advantageous sites those who were to till the soil.

In another part of the continent, Judah Touro entered upon a distinguished career in a different branch of trade. Touro had been born in Newport in 1775, just as that thriving community was about to be dispersed by the Revolution. He made his way to Boston where he served as an apprentice to his uncle, a merchant. At fourteen, he went as supercargo on a voyage to the Mediterranean, and in the next ten years engaged in a variety of business ventures.

In 1802 Touro came to New Orleans and determined to stay there. The port at the mouth of the Mississippi was then on the verge of a sudden change in its fortunes. Traded back and forth between France and Spain, it had been cut off from the backcountry for which it was the natural marketplace. Then, in 1803, it passed into American hands along with the Louisiana Purchase and entered upon a period of steady development. Thereafter all the products of the expanding West moved down the Ohio and Mississippi to pass through New Orleans counting houses to be exchanged for the wares of Europe and the East.

In this setting Touro's business flourished; his connections were world-wide and his ventures many. Yet he also had time to serve his community actively, to bear arms in the War of 1812, and to build friendships of lifelong intimacy. His career is one of many that showed how deeply Jews had struck roots in the United States.

This adjustment determined the character of Jewish communal life. The tone of familiarity with which they participated in the activities of the country, the free and easy intercourse with their fellow citizens, profoundly altered the group's view of itself. The European Jews' conception of an integrated community, decisively separated from the society around it, had already faded in 1770, and it disappeared shortly thereafter. The great majority of Jews were natives and thought themselves wholly a part of their society. They drew off to themselves, as did other Americans, only in particular voluntary activities that affected the group alone.

Thus the Jews entered into the communal life about them as equals and without the least appearance of separateness. Politically, they often held public office. They moved without self-consciousness in polite society and were prominent in the Masonic order; Moses Michael Hays between 1788 and 1792 was Grand Master of the Massachusetts Grand Lodge. Occasional intermarriage continued to reveal the closeness of these contacts, and also the equality of the faiths, for such alliances did not always result in alienation from the Jewish community.

At the points at which Jews perceived separate organizations to be desirable, they nevertheless felt no compulsion to draw together into any unified entity. In religious matters, for instance, the synagogue was no longer coterminous with the community, for it had ceased to be an agency of all Jews and had become a voluntary organization created by some of them. In some cities there was more than one congregation; and in others a sprinkling of new philanthropic and educational institutions arose, altogether unconnected with the synagogue. The school of the Congregation Shearith Israel of New York, in existence since 1731, in 1802 acquired an identity of its own when it was established as the Polonies Talmud Torah. Significant indications of the fragmentation of the functions of the traditional *Kahal*, or congregation, appeared elsewhere in the same period.

By 1820 the Jews of the United States in their experiences as individuals also encountered the challenge of these novel conditions. Three lives reveal in their varied responses the extent to which these people had been integrated with their society, retaining their faith as Jews and living fully as Americans.

Thomas Sully, a facile portrait painter, settled in Philadelphia in 1810. He had no difficulty securing commissions, and he turned his paintings out with skill. He had an eye for feminine character, perhaps because his early years had been spent among touring companies of actor in the South. One of his subjects he found particularly impressive. Her "easy pose suggestive of perfect health," her delicately turned neck and "firmly poised head," her "fine white skin and firmly chiseled nose" exhausted his store of adjectives. In her person there was "all that a princess of the blood Royal might have coveted." All these attributes left him with "no doubt as to the race from which she had sprung."

Rebecca Gratz's ability to captivate men's imaginations was not limited to those she met face to face. Her charm could be conveyed in words spoken beyond the ocean. Visiting in Scotland, Washington Irving spoke of her to Sir Walter Scott, who was so taken with the description that he made her the heroine of *Ivanhoe*.

In Sully's portrait she confronts us still, a nice girl, placidly smiling, with her somewhat plain face set off by the modish turban on her head. Her letters reveal a good soul, occupied with works of benevolence and alive to the intellectual and cultural currents of her time. She never married.

Why then the excess of enthusiasm? Rebecca Gratz of Philadelphia was the symbol of a new and exciting personality. The figure of the beautiful, noble Jewess had been known in English literature since Shakespeare's Jessica; conventionally

she had been eager to escape from the restrictions of the
ghetto to the freedom of the Christian world outside it. But
Rebecca was untrammeled either by ghetto restrictions or by
inherited bias. Instead she was the modern woman, with an
identity and a will of her own, capable of moving with ease
and grace through the fashionable salons of the time. Yet she
remained a Jewess, and without tormenting doubts or conflict.

Her contemporary, Mordecai Manuel Noah, also a Phila-
delphian, turned a corner of his life and unexpectedly ran into
an ancient source of strife. His reaction was characteristically
American.

Noah was native-born, raised and educated first in Philadelphia. He was a Jew, but consciousness of his identity rode
lightly upon him. He came to New York to follow a journalist's career, and then tried his hand at playwriting, and with
moderate success dabbled in politics. A Democrat, the quirks
of party maneuvering gave him the nomination for county
sheriff. Here and there qualms were expressed: was it proper
to put a Jew in an office that might give him the opportunity
to hang a Christian? A more pertinent question resolved the
doubts: what kind of Christian was it that deserved to be
hanged? In any case, Noah was elected and served his term.

In due course political service led Noah to the more lucra-
tive rewards of office. In 1813 President Madison appointed
him American consul at Tunis. Traveling through North
Africa, Noah for the first time beheld Jews who were not
Americans. The sight of the poverty and oppression, the degradation and helplessness of his co-religionists shocked and
outraged the American. No doubt he was naïve; such inferior-

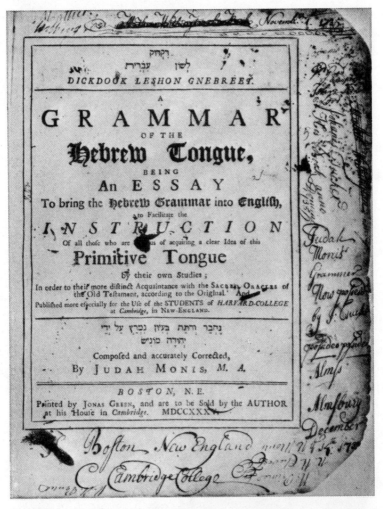

The title page for the first work of Jewish learning in the United States. The work was a Hebrew grammar printed in 1735 and "sold by the author at his house in Cambridge." Its author, Judah Monis, was a tutor at Harvard College and his grammar was used by students of the Hebrew language there.

Mordecai Manuel Noah (above) of Philadelphia, appointed American consul at Tunis in 1813 by President Madison, was horrified by the poverty and degradation of his fellow Jews in North Africa. . . . Judah Tuoro, whose business in international trade thrived in New Orleans during the first two decades of the nineteenth century. (Courtesy of Redwood Library, Newport, R.I.)

ity, to some degree, was the normal state of Jews everywhere but in the United States. Nevertheless, the memory rankled. Noah would long be horrified by the evidence of the extent to which the lot of the Jews in the New World differed from that elsewhere.

Noah returned to America determined to do something, his determination no doubt heightened by the suspicion that he may have lost his post through the unwillingness of the Moslem ruler of Tunis to deal with a Jewish emissary. A number of fanciful visions flitted through Noah's mind, and a grandiose scheme finally emerged. He would himself redeem the depressed; and he would do so through all the opportunities America afforded.

In some available part of the United States, Noah planned to gather thousands of Jews from all parts of the world to prepare for the eventual Messianic return to Palestine. Practical considerations mingled with the ideal as he moved to implement this fantastic plan. On Grand Island, in the vicinity of Buffalo, he hoped to prepare a colony to receive the newcomers; perhaps there he might also profit through the sale of real estate. In 1825, in the Episcopal Church of Buffalo, he dedicated the new settlement, to be known as Ararat, and addressed a message to the Jews of the world, inviting them to his "city of refuge."

Nothing came of all this. The episode was significant not for its results but for the attitudes it revealed. Noah's reactions to North Africa had their source in a continuing sense of responsibility toward the Jews of the rest of the world. And he was so at home in America, that the ingathering there of all the persecuted seemed to him the logical mode of relief.

In a very similar community at almost the same time, Isaac Harby gave considerable thought to the modus of religious adjustment to American life. Charleston, South Carolina, was already a thriving town, growing with the trade of its prosperous backcountry. It prided itself also on a tradition of culture and upon its cultivated, leisurely manner of life. The Jews of the city were comfortable and confident. They had had a synagogue since 1750 and were growing steadily in numbers. Active in trade and in the cultural and intellectual affairs of the city, it is not surprising that they pondered the means by which their Judaism could be embodied in forms more like those of their neighbors. The young people particularly wished some alterations in the traditional orthodoxy of the ritual of religious worship. They were sometimes offended by the old-fashioned auctioning-off of places in the service; they did not understand the loud and familiar tones in which their elders addressed their God; they saw no sense to the continued use of Spanish in the ritual; and they wanted the reader to deliver a sermon in English "like all other ministers." In a word, they did not see why they should not conform to the outward practices of the other American sects.

In 1824 forty-seven members of the local congregation petitioned for changes along these lines, and when the petition was rejected, constituted themselves the Reformed Society of Israelites in South Carolina, to worship by the new mode. Harby was among the leaders of the movement. He was then not yet forty, a thoughtful but unsettled man whose career had led him to teaching, the drama, the law, and journalism. His earnest questioning gave impetus to the discontent that led to the organization of the Society; and his *Discourse* a year later expressed its desire to achieve a conciliation between Judaism and American religious liberalism.

The society was not long-lived. Its brief appearance at this relatively early date was nevertheless indicative of the degree to which Judaism had become Americanized. A population increasingly native in composition had moved away from its European antecedents and had become impatient with the practices saddled upon them by the past.

Across the ocean, meanwhile, there were being readied forces of enormous power that would displace millions of Europeans, among them the Jews. Before many years went by, the effects of the displacement would be felt in the United States and would then help fundamentally to reshape the patterns of life that had begun to emerge under the early republic.

CHAPTER THREE

The Problems of an Expanding Society

After 1820 a succession of disturbing shocks disordered the placid course of American development. The end result would be growth of a magnitude never before anticipated. Through the next fifty years the nation was destined to suffer the painful necessity of adjusting itself to the new circumstances created by its own expansion and by the arrival of some seven and a half million immigrants to its shores.

Jews, along with other Americans, encountered the massive problems of national expansion. But they, like the Catholics and Lutherans, faced additional perplexities with the knowledge that among these newcomers to the United States were thousands of their own co-religionists. Like Noah, but on a larger scale, they discovered, by contact with the Jews of the Old World, how far different they themselves had become. In the next five troubled decades, the old settlers and the new arrivals learned to know one another, and to develop together an American pattern of communal life.

Jewish immigration, after 1820, no longer involved mere handfuls of individuals, carried along by the tow of individual circumstances. It was now a mass movement, its sweep derived from sources general to the whole European continent.

After 1820, with few exceptions, the Jews who left their old homes to make new ones for themselves in the United States came from Europe, but from a milieu different from that of the seventeenth-century arrivals. Nor were the immigrants of these years in any sense homogeneous as a group. Long centuries of development had cut apart the various remnants of Israel that survived in all parts of the continent, had perpetuated differences in customs and in position, and had left their mark in diversities that would be carried across the ocean to influence the growth of the community in America.

Such divisions are not at all simple of definition. Every hamlet had its local peculiarities, every region its distinctive singularity. Often, in the New World, these immediate local differences were as important in the practical life of the immigrants as the more obvious lines of national or linguistic division. Traditionally, however, the Jews of Europe themselves accepted a number of major demarcations. The old separation of Sephardic and Ashkenazic communities was still recognized and, in some places, was even buttressed by support of the law. Small numbers of Sephardic Jews survived in western Europe—in France, in Holland, in England, in Germany—as well as in southeastern Europe. Tracing their ancestry to Spanish and Portuguese exiles, these people in the west were low in number and high in social and economic status. From among them had come the first migrants to the New World. Now, in the nineteenth century, they had achieved a stable way of life where they were; and they did not enter the new streams of migration significantly.

The world of Ashkenazic (German) Jewry was divided, in the closing years of the eighteenth century, into two main areas of settlement. A small minority lived in the west—in France and the Low Countries, in England and in southern Germany. A great majority, perhaps 80 per cent, lived in lands that were, at one time or another, part of the Kingdom of Poland—Poland itself, Lithuania, White Russia, and the Ukraine —and in the neighboring fringes of Hungary and Romania.

The differences, in the eighteenth century, between the Jews of the west and those of the east were not geographic alone. The whole context of life in the two areas was dissimilar to a degree that markedly affected the social and cultural structure of each group.

At root was a fundamental divergence in economic experience. In the west, long generations of enforced residence in a ghetto had defined the status of the Jews. There they were confined to a limited number of occupations, to usury and its accompanying forms of retailing—pawnbrokering and the sale of secondhand goods. Generally, restrictions by the guilds kept these people out of the handicraft industries, and the hostility of the established merchants shut them off from the more remunerative forms of trade. From agriculture they were entirely excluded.

In the east, on the other hand, the position of the Jews was more open. The golden age of Polish Jewry had come to a close in the seventeenth century. The furious uprising of Chmielnicki's Cossacks in 1648 had all but destroyed them; as the savage horsemen from the Dnieper frontier had blazed across the countryside, their bitterness against their Polish overlords had largely been vented against the helpless Jews.

A century later, marks of that disaster still scarred the communities of eastern Europe. Yet in the eighteenth century, the economy of the east continued to offer the Jews a range of useful functions. No compulsory ghetto existed there. Unlike the west, society was still dominated by a manorial system of production. Emphasis on subsistence agriculture, in a society not accustomed to much trade, perpetuated a population that was overwhelmingly rural, a mass of peasants and a sprinkling of noble landlords. Without a competing indigenous middle class, the Jews were free to enter a wide range of occupations, and managed to make a living, although they rarely prospered, in the various branches of industry and commerce.

A significant divergence in religious experience complimented the divergence in economic position. The narrow life of the western ghetto, walled off from the rest of society, had set the conditions for a rigid religious formalism, dominated by corporate communities, highly organized and controlled by the state. The Jews of the east were no less orthodox, but their orthodoxy was not divorced from the whole life of the world in which they lived. The relatively free and favorable conditions which existed until the uprising of the Cossacks in 1648 had nurtured a rich communal life with a culture meaningfully oriented around religion. In the secure round of existence of the *shtetl*, the little Jewish town, men had been able to guide their every action by a pattern of divinely ordained precepts that endowed their behavior with a pervasive aura of holiness. From the seats of the scholars in the centers of learning to the humble cottages of the water carriers and craftsmen, there was a continuity of faith and a sense of wholeness in the universe.

Conditions in the east were less free and less favorable after the disasters of the mid-seventeenth century when a steady deterioration in this way of life set in. The Cossacks moved away; but from the rubble they left behind, arose a miasma that thereafter sickened the spirits of those Jews who remained. In the poisoned atmosphere, minds deprived of other hopes were set to incessant reverie; vague fanciful dreams took shape of some mystic redemption, of some magic solution to the intolerable problems for which no earthly solution was apparent. Now a line of messiahs appeared, from Shabbathai Zebi to Jacob Frank, who led thousands of deluded followers to the heights of ecstasy and then plunged them into black despair.

For a time Chasidism, a popular movement stressing personal piety and mysticism, offered a measure of compensation. The environment, physical and human, was often harsh and disorderly, oppression and bitterness were no strangers. Yet even here, taught the Baal Shem Tov (Master of the Good Name) and his followers, God was omnipresent, spreading over the least action the warmth of His holiness. Even the least of men, even the poorest and most ignorant, could discover the joy of His lovingkindness by faithful adherence to His precepts.

In this realm of small villages, of nobles and of peasants, Chasidism made of Jewishness more than a yoke thrust on from without; faith now became a way to God that transcended all mundane distinctions. By 1750 Chasidism had spread its influence to every part of eastern Europe, so deep was the longing of the people for reassurance.

Only this consolation too was short-lived. The spirit of the early mystics did not animate their successors. The *Zaddik*, or *Chasidic* leader, became a holy man, living in luxurious courts off the tribute of his miserable followers. Meanwhile the mass of Jews sank deeper into an apathetic despair than ever before, while their beliefs became entangled in a moldy web of superstition in which the evil eye, spells and incantations, messianic illusions, and traditional precepts were hopelessly entangled.

As the eighteenth century drew to a close, neither the Jews of the east nor those of the west seemed in a position to break out of the constricted life to which history had consigned them. Yet in both areas, the nineteenth century would be a time of sweeping change, which would set millions of these Jews free and on the move—a large part of them toward the United States.

In the west, a new era seemed already to have dawned in the glow of the enlightenment. The first signs came in fields that were broadly cultural and intellectual. The fresh currents of eighteenth-century ideas of natural human goodness and natural human rights tended to minimize religious differences and to stress instead common ethical principles. In a reciprocal influence that would last more than a century, Christian thinkers stressed the rights of Jews to equality, while Jews of all ranks found increasingly attractive and increasingly accessible the whole world of non-Jewish thought and activity.

The cultural walls between Jew and gentile had hardly been breached when the ghetto itself was razed. Out of the French Revolution came a series of radical impulses that everywhere in western Europe transformed the place of the Jews in society. To begin with, the conception of natural rights left no basis for justifying the invidious discriminations under which Jews labored. Furthermore, a new view of nationality emerged from the Revolution and in that view there was no place for the separate, autonomous communities in which the Jews had once lived. Citizenship was tied to nationality, and whatever differences were considered to exist between Jews and other citizens were deemed to be religious only. Jews ceased to occupy a special position as members of a national community within the territory of France and Germany; they became Frenchmen and Germans of the Jewish religion. At the same time, church and state were progressively being separated, and a new tolerance gave these citizens all the rights of their neighbors. The transformation did not come at once. But the trend was unmistakable and steadily worked itself out in France and England, in Germany and in the Austrian empire.

Emancipation in this political sense was accompanied by relaxation of many economic restrictions. A wide range of new opportunities opened up to the Jews. The Revolution in France, and the aftermath of revolution in the rest of western Europe, destroyed the power of the old guilds and enabled the Jews to enter many forms of enterprise hitherto closed to them. Meanwhile, unparalleled economic growth in trade and in industry created a state of flux in which there was the opportunity for improvement of the material condition of the Jews.

These changes were not confined to the political limits of the western European states; their influence permeated eastward through the whole of the continent. The times were propitious for change. By now, the Jews of the east were entering upon a long period of instability and uncertainty. Their position was decidedly weakened by the decline of the old economic order and by the rise of trade, which brought with it a competing Christian middle class.

Partition of the Kingdom of Poland in the last quarter of the eighteenth century further threatened the security of the Jews in the east. The largest portion of eastern Jewry then fell under the sway of the Czar, and the Romanov autocrat was not disposed to make the concessions that had once been granted by the laxer regimes of Poland, Lithuania, and the Ukraine.

While this partition of Poland subjected so many to Russia, it also brought a portion of eastern Jewry under the sovereignty of German rulers who, at that very time, were ameliorating the condition of their subjects. In Prussian Posen, in Austrian Galicia, large bodies of eastern Jews became conscious of the advantages of what was happening in the west. Through them, the western influences were transmitted eastward, all the way across the border into Russia.

The attractiveness of the new conditions in the west, coinciding with the deterioration of the situation in the east, created a magnetic pull that drew large numbers of Jews from the east through Germany to France and England, through Bohemia and Hungary to the heart of Austria, and through Romania southward. Emigration was, of course, easiest from the Polish provinces of Prussia and Austria, but it was by no means confined to these regions, for until almost the end of the nineteenth century political boundaries were not serious barriers to the enterprising.

Furthermore, the same changes generated an intellectual

force that spread eastward and began to affect those Jews who remained in their old homes. The new economic and cultural conditions were weakening the old communal institutions and were provoking thought as to what should be the situation of the Jews in the modern world. Now it seemed as if, at last, the Jews would no longer be destined to remain isolated, would come to grips with all the social and intellectual problems of modern life. The ideas of the enlightenment, of the *haskalah*, spread eastward and slowly penetrated into all the districts of Jewry. In the west, the ghetto walls had crumbled and it would not be long before the integrity of the Jewish community was similarly disrupted in the farthest reaches of Poland, White Russia, and the Ukraine.

These events did not transpire in a vacuum. The Jews were no longer isolated and did not escape the effects of very general economic pressures that were coming to play upon the whole society in which they lived. Beginning in England late in the eighteenth century, and then spreading through France and Germany to central and eastern Europe, a profound revolution reorganized the industrial life of the continent. Everywhere, great capitalist factories manned by a wage-earning proletariat, and run by power, replaced the old independent workshop of the artisan who toiled by hand. Everywhere, large farms, operated by hired labor and machines, took the place of the small peasant holdings. A vast network of railroads and steamship lines, a complicated commercial and credit system, began to knit together the outlines of a new world economy.

The shock of these cataclysmic transformations jolted millions of people out of their accustomed positions. First to be displaced were the artisans whose skills lost their values as more efficient mechanical competitors turned out enormous quantities of cheap goods. The artisans were followed, usually after a decade or so, by peasants, ejected from the ancestral acres of their masters to make way for more effective techniques of production. All of these uprooted persons had to find new homes, some in the rising cities, others, across the seas in foreign lands.

The Jews, too, were affected by the change. Their old economic position, precarious at best, and in any case changing, quickly became altogether untenable. For under the conditions of the transformed system of production, the Jews could not maintain their accustomed role. In the west, many farmers, artisans, and petty retailers in the small towns—the Jews among them—were compelled to change their way of making a living. In the east, as the peasants were displaced, the Jews, who lived by dealing with them, became superfluous.

But this general economic change was far from the only difficulty. Not only was there less opportunity where they were but, at the very same time, the number of Jews grew phenomenally, at a rate higher than the incredible increase in the total population. The two million Jews estimated to live in Europe in 1800 more than tripled in the course of the century that followed, and continued to grow in the three decades after 1900, despite losses by emigration, disasters, war, pogroms, conversion, and intermarriage.

With more hands and less need of them in the old towns and villages, some movement was inevitable if whole communities were not to sink further into abject poverty. But before large masses of people were willing to migrate, the bonds that tied them to the places where they were born had to be loosened. In a psychological sense, that was achieved by the enlightenment that freed many Jews from the forces of local communal authority. Emancipation, or even the consciousness that emancipation was possible, generated a desire for improvement that sometimes amounted to a virulent fever and infected whole districts. In a physical sense it was achieved by the growth of trade and the spread of railroads and shipping lines that made movement easier.

The impact both of the enlightenment and of the growth of trade, as well as of the underlying economic changes, was felt first in the west and then in the east. The displacement of people followed the same order, coming earliest at the English Channel, and latest in the Czar's domain.

The transfer of Jewish population was, however, no simple matter. Actually three distinct currents were involved. First was a migration from small towns to the large cities where the new commercial and industrial opportunities were to be found. In the nineteenth century, large Jewish agglomerations were built up in London and Paris, Berlin and Vienna, Budapest and Bucharest, Lodz and Warsaw, Odessa and Kharkov. The seven largest German cities in 1816 held 7 per cent of the Jews in the country, 50 per cent a hundred years later. At the same time, there was a shift of population from east to west, from the less to the more developed industrial regions. The century saw a substantial rise in the number of foreign Jews in England, France, and Germany.

But in the midst of all this shuffling about, some Jews turned their minds to a break that was more complete. These people had had enough of the Old World and were eager to find a new. Perhaps a taste of emancipation and enlightenment had shown them there was not emancipation or enlightenment enough in Europe. Certainly opportunities were more readily to be found across the Atlantic. Increasingly, those who sought a change found it by leaving the continent altogether.

These were the elemental forces that carried the flow of Jewish immigrants to America. Occasionally specific local conditions accelerated or retarded the movement. Political and civic discrimination, such as the limitation upon the number of Jewish marriages in Bavaria, stimulated the exodus from southwestern Germany in the 1840s. The failure of the revolutions of 1848 in central Europe set others on the move. But such incidental factors did not significantly alter the general contours of the movement.

In the half-century before 1870, this emigration to America was generally western, not in the sense that the emigrants were all natives of western states, but in the sense that they were dominated by western, and particularly by German, influences. Whatever the nationality of these Jews, they either lived under German monarchs, or unavoidably spent a greater or lesser period in some German state in the process of transit, or had been swayed by German conceptions of emancipation in the course of breaking with the Old World.

In this period the total number of Jewish immigrants was somewhere between two and four hundred thousand in all. (The statistics of immigration in these years are hopelessly inaccurate; any more specific figure is no more than a guess.) This inflow raised the total Jewish population of the United States from perhaps 5,000 in 1820 to 20,000 in 1848, and to several hundred thousand (some say two, some say as much as six) in 1870. Growth at so rapid a rate imposed upon the Jews already established in the United States the necessity of radical adjustments. Those adjustments came within the context of changes in the whole society of which they were a part.

All America was being transformed in these years. Between 1820 and 1870 the population of the country quadrupled, from ten to nearly forty million. At the start of the period, the bulk of the population was confined to the area east of the Alleghenies with advance outpourings along the lines of the Mohawk and Ohio Rivers and at the mouth of the Mississippi. By the end of the period a vast domain had been settled that reached well west of the Mississippi, through Minnesota, Kanas, and Nebraska to the interior of Texas, with a substantial outpost along the Pacific Coast.

In large part the migration consisted of people who intended agriculture to be their lives; the enormous increase in the production of wheat, corn, cotton, and other crops, after 1820, testified to the effect of their movement. Yet these were not such farmers as could live cut off from the world. In their advance, they depended upon the extension into the new areas of immensely improved means of communication. They themselves moved Westward, as did later the goods they consumed, along a complex network of roads, canals, and railroads. In time the same network would also carry the products of their fields to the East and to foreign markets. At the crucial points of interchange there sprang up numerous trading towns to handle the flow of goods.

The enormous expansion of agriculture went hand in hand with the creation of a new industrial system. In the Northeast and in many parts of the Middle West the growing markets, available capital, and the labor of new immigrant hands, stimulated the rapid development of manufacturing. In the decade of the Civil War, the United States was already able to supply many of its domestic requirements for manufactured goods, and was well on the way to being an exporter of them.

This dazzling economic growth set the terms and created the conditions under which the hosts of the newcoming Jews would adjust themselves. For, to these people, as to all immigrants, the problems of economic adaptation were most crucial.

A very few Jews were among the representatives of European banking houses that extended their operations to the New World in the period just around the Civil War. But most Jews, like most other immigrants, were not so fortunate. They rarely came with substantial stores of capital, and seldom had direct personal or business connections in America. How well off they were at the start may be gauged by the fact that in the 1850s between 10 and 20 per cent of those in New York were assisted by the Jewish charities. For all these people the first concern had to be finding a way to earn a livelihood. All had to cope quickly with the problem of how to adapt the skills and training of the Old World to the need of making a living under the strange conditions of the New.

Among the migrants of this half-century were many who had been accustomed to carrying on trade at home, either in the west as petty retailers, or in the east as intermediaries between the life of the peasants and the life of the towns. Many of these people found opportunities for similar kinds of business in the United States.

The simplest commerce was that transacted from out of the

peddler's pack. The conduct of such an enterprise required little capital, and only the ability to work hard for a slight margin of return. The peddler found his most accessible market among other immigrants, who were accustomed in Europe to dealing in this manner with itinerant traders, and who were reluctant to enter into complicated relationships with the more formal, one-price, native shops and stores. Later he extended his clientele, took in other residents of the city.

Above all, he carried his trade to the people who lived on farms, people who had some money to spend but little opportunity for travel to distant cities. Everywhere through the West the rapid march of settlement outdistanced the ability of the towns to supply the rural districts with needed goods. And in the South and East there remained a continuing demand for the wares of the itinerant merchandisers. Landing in the various seaports along the Atlantic Coast, the Jewish peddler soon got his start and made his way into the interior where he became a familiar figure, matching his wares and wits with Yankee, Irish, and German competitors. Now and then one of them, like John Meyer Levy of LaCrosse, found his livelihood as an Indian trader.

We will never know how many of these itinerant peddlers barely scraped by without ever advancing in wealth, grew old without security; and how many more were failures, forced back upon charity, men who joined the ranks of the *schnorrers*, the beggars, the tramps, the hoboes, who wandered from town to town, living by gifts of the local synagogues anxious to be rid of them. Generally we hear only of the more fortunate.

The successful found this mode of life a temporary expedient and soon accumulated surplus enough to transform the pack into a settled retail establishment. There was certainly room for such undertakings under the conditions of the American economy. The Westward movement yearly created scores of new towns that were eager to be served in this manner, places where newly arrived merchants were more than welcome. Often in his journeyings the wandering peddler hit upon just such a likely place, decided to stay, and sent for his family. It was not long before the length and breadth of the land was dotted with general stores and groceries, dry-goods stores and some not so dry, shoe, clothing, hardware, and every other kind of establishment.

Merchants also found similar opportunities in the expanding cities. Here too there was growth and a demand for new services. As the heart of the city became more densely populated and as the city itself spread outward, engulfing suburb after suburb, the whole pattern of retail trading changed, and immigrant shopkeepers played an important role in that change. Some commodities—dry goods, for instance—had always been distributed through retail establishments; there was now more demand for dealers in such products. But many other articles had not been exchanged in this manner. Food and fuel had been brought by farmers directly to markets where consumers could come and buy. Most articles of clothing and furniture were made to order. To buy such commodities, only the poor, who were willing to wear and use secondhand goods, went to a shop where the cast-off, the misfit, and the un-fresh were stored. Since the poor were mostly immigrants who preferred to trade with other immigrants and since, in any case, natives shunned such peripheral trades, the secondhand shops were kept by immigrants, among them the Jews.

Expansion of the cities, however, made many other people dependent upon the same shops. Sooner or later, local farmers would no longer be able to bring their produce to market, for many foodstuffs came from far-off places; houses were smaller and had less storage space; and ready-made replaced custom-made articles. The business of the shopkeeper increased enormously; and, in this case, the immigrant was there first and thrived correspondingly. This development, continuing throughout the nineteenth century, created attractive new opportunities for scores of arriving Jews.

In relatively short order a substantial number of Jews acquired comfortable positions. While few rose to be among the wealthiest Americans, some did move toward the upper mercantile ranks, acting as brokers or merchants after the colonial pattern. In 1848, for instance, the Seligman brothers had been operating a dry-goods store in Alabama for several years. Seeking wider opportunities, they divided. Joseph, William, and James moved to New York City where they embarked upon the clothing business. Meanwhile Jesse went by way of Watertown, New York, to San Francisco, where his general store prospered. In 1857 the brothers were reunited in New York, their firm now an imposing brokerage house. Five years later they were bankers, soon with branches in Frankfort, London, and Paris.

More significant, however, was the range of moderate opportunities the developing economy opened to many newcomers. The little shops, modest on their own account, added up to an impressive total; by 1847, it was estimated that 25 per cent of New York's dry-goods sales were by Jews.

The absence of comparable opportunities accounts for the fact that industry now attracted relatively few. Occasionally one or another would find that the nature of his trade led him into manufacturing. Thus Levi Strauss, a peddler among the California miners, hit upon a device to give his trousers exceptional strength. With the aid of a local tailor he began to make and sell his own; soon knowing Westerners would accept none but Levi's, and the business was well established.

But in general, the structure of American industry was discouraging to newcomers. In manufacturing, only two roles were possible: that of laborer from which there was no opportunity of advancement; and that of capitalist, which called for a surplus for investment. On neither count were the Jews attracted. Wherever possible they avoided the dead end of the proletarian's status; and their small stores of capital could more advantageously be invested in trade.

Somewhat similar reasons explained their absence from agriculture. Jews, then and later, attached great importance to the cultivation of the soil. Through these years projects rose and fell which drew off a few of these newcomers to settlement on the land. Noah's Ararat flickered in hope for a brief interval in the 1820s, and a decade later the Association Zeire Hazon ambitiously indulged in the same dream. Moses Cohen's Shalom in Ulster County, New York, actually came into existence for a few years in the 1840s. So, too, in 1843 Julius Stern contrived a great scheme for bringing his co-religionists to farming; and eight years later B'nai B'rith sponsored the

Hebrew Agricultural Society to aid such would-be husbandmen.

All such efforts came to naught. Nor did the Jew as an individual often make his way to a farm on his own. He lacked the training and the skill to become a frontiersman; the ax, the gun, and the ability to live off the soil were alike strange to him. Yet, to settle down in an area already developed, to buy land already cleared, required capital which he did not have. Sometimes such a man labored and saved, intending some day to be lord of his own plot. Usually, when the balance became large enough, he found it more profitable and more consistent with his own skills to invest in trade.

The nature of the economic adjustment was basic in influencing the forms of Jewish settlement in the United States. It was not dislike for distance that had kept the Jews off the farm. Indeed, every now and then one of them, like S. N. Carvalho, who accompanied Frémont to the Rocky Mountains, found himself in the vanguard of an exploring expedition. Where trade took them, they would go.

Trade took them everywhere, on foot, on horseback, by ship, in covered wagon. In many a small Southern or Western town, two or three Jewish families brought the routes of trade to the vicinity of the farm. No city of any size lacked Jews. In the mining camps of California they were familiar figures; and the Mormon columns had not long come to rest in Utah before the Jews appeared in Salt Lake City. Consequently the newcomers were inclined to disperse through the length and breadth of the country rather than to concentrate in a few large places, although there were, as might be expected, heavy accumulations in the oldest cities.

The high degree of dispersal and relative prosperity of the group accounted for the ease of its adaptation to American life. The Jews in this period evaded the most difficult urban problems. They faced the initial necessity of taking care of poor newcomers just off the boat. But unlike the Irish and some of the Germans who immigrated at the same period, they were not permanently plagued by unemployment and pauperism, nor by overcrowding and slum housing, disease, crime, and delinquency that were the concomitants of poverty.

On the contrary, the Jews entered untroubled into the main currents of the society about them. A few earned prominence. Joseph Goldmark gained an enviable reputation as a physician; and Ernestine L. Rose participated vigorously in the abolition movement, women's rights, and in other reform activities of the 1840s and 1850s. But by and large the Jews did not particularly distinguish themselves in the arts, the sciences, or the professions. Nor did they now figure notably in politics.

That was, however, the result of abstention not exclusion; trade and settlement monopolized the group's energies. There were few expressions of hostility toward the Jews, and no disposition by others to limit their participation in the life of the nation. Debates over religious rights in this period centered on such matters as the Sunday laws and the sectarian wording of Thanksgiving proclamations. Only a few zealous nativists protested against continued immigration, and one of them, Lewis C. Levin, was himself a Jew. Such prejudices, however, were abhorrent to most Americans, as was clearly demonstrated in 1840 in the reaction to the raising of the blood libel against the Jews of Damascus. The revival, five thousand miles away, of the ancient accusation that the blood of a Christian child was required for the Passover ritual was greeted in the United States with a wave of protests by men of every religion.

The Civil War tested Jewish adjustment to America, and on the whole these folk reacted to the great conflict exactly as did their neighbors. In the North, despite the fact that many had been members of the Democratic Party, they actively supported the war; in the South, they were equally loyal supporters of the Confederacy. Some Jews had earlier defended the slaveholders, and others the abolitionists. August Bondi fought with John Brown in Kansas, and Judah P. Benjamin was Secretary of War for Jefferson Davis. In both cases, their actions were determined by forces common to the whole community in which they lived.

Indeed, the largest problems of adjustment in these years came not from the relationship of Jews to the society around them but from their relationship to one another. The new immigration had been at once upsetting and stimulating, and the evolving patterns of communal life showed the effects of that disturbance.

CHAPTER FOUR

The Pattern of American Communal Life

The migrants of the half-century after 1820 came into a society extremely fluid in its patterns of organization. The Jewish community they encountered was small in size, and had already begun radically to depart from its traditional orthodox past. The newcomers by their numbers soon outweighed those on the spot and, by the particular problems of their situation, gave a new turn to the earlier trends.

These adjustments throw light on the role of institutional activity in Jewish life. Emigration had destroyed the inner meaning of the whole pattern of the traditional Jewish community. On this unfamiliar ground old forms, no longer appropriate, were, willingly or not, readapted, sometimes discarded and replaced. This foreign land, which was doubly foreign because for some it was also an urban land, challenged the newcomer to make here a new mode of living.

Those who settled in the very largest cities were able to create whatever institutions their needs demanded. But the majority, dispersed in the interior in much smaller units of settlement, turned to one expedient after another to compensate for lack of numbers. In the small towns the Jews did not settle as a coherent residential group, or if they did, quickly flew apart as they become able to improve their living quarters. Here only the synagogue and a few subordinate institutions— cemeteries, mutual assistance societies, and the like—drew the community together. Strict orthodox observance was difficult, and those who were not religious lost all contact with the Jewish community.

The extreme situation existed in thousands of places where Jews settled in such small numbers that it was difficult to assemble a bare *minyan* (ritual group of ten men, necessary for worship), and where the struggle to maintain a synagogue exhausted all communal energies. For many lonely ones, so isolated, Jewishness faded into a thin memory of antecedents, revived, from time to time, by little visits to the big cities.

Even less successfully than other men could the immigrant live alone. Surrounded by strangers and oppressed by the constant risk of being left helpless, he had no well-established roots to hold him up in adversity. He turned, as a matter of course, to his fellows, seeking with them to contrive organizations that would strengthen his hand against an alien world.

Such organizations played a twofold role. They set up an area of activity in which the immigrant could meet and relax, away from the critical gaze of outsiders, in the company of people like himself. Here he could win the friendship of people whose esteem he valued, become a person of importance, a president, an officer. Here could be found solidarity of values and the sympathetic judgment of personalities. The same organizations also performed specific religious, social, and charitable functions useful in the lives of their members. So, when a group came together, they formed a *chevra*, a company, a guild, for common action toward common ends.

Of course, those who came to the Atlantic seaboard cities found in existence by the 1820s well-established synagogues which they were expected to join. But these had a character of their own, not always acceptable to the new arrivals. Such places of worship were controlled by native American Jews whose customs diverged significantly from those of Jews in the old country. American congregations were accustomed from colonial times to follow the lead of their English counterparts; they used the Sephardic ritual, they received advice on moot questions from London or Amsterdam, and wrote there for recommendations when they sought a minister. The old synagogues persisted in these practices through the period and thereby alienated the newcomers.

Furthermore, the Americans consistently had a reputation for impiety among immigrants, at whatever date the latter arrived; in the United States, it was thought, people did not observe the Sabbath in its full strictness; they gave up European dress too quickly; they shaved; they were careless in observing the dietary laws of *kashruth;* and they were ignorant of the Torah, not even having rabbis to guide them. No wonder the newly arrived Jew would be suspicious of them!

The first synagogues attempted to maintain a monopolistic position. That in Charleston, for instance, ruled that no unauthorized *minyan* could gather within a radius of five miles. But there were no means of enforcing such arbitrary legislation, for unlike some European communities, these did not have the support of the state. The synagogue was entirely under lay control and there was neither rabbinate nor any other body to exercise discipline. Any group that liked could assemble in a *chevra* and worship God to its heart's content and in its own way. In Georgia such a schism had already appeared before the Revolution.

In the smallest places there was no choice; the few Jews "scattered through the wilds of America" clung together out of necessity, whatever the divergencies among them. But a community did not have to be very large to indulge in the luxury of internal division. New synagogues appeared as soon as the growth of population made it possible to support them. Sometimes, as in 1825 when B'nai Jeshurun was organized in New York, the motives were concerned with religious considerations; the organizers then wished to follow the "rites, custom, and usage of the German and Polish Jews" and to free themselves from contact with those who violated the Sabbath. Sometimes the motives were more personal: a conflict over elections, an offense to someone's dignity, or a dispute over the hiring of a cantor. But one way or another, the number of congregations grew, "forming factions, clans, small corporations." By the outbreak of the Civil War, there were in New York, in addition to the old American group, German, Polish, Dutch, English, Bohemian, and Russian congregations; and Cincinnati, Philadelphia, and other cities witnessed a similar proliferation.

These nationalistic designations did not necessarily refer to the nativity of the members; a correspondent of the *Israelite* in 1856 pointed out, "the so-called Polish Congregation consists of Polanders, Hollanders, English, German and other nations." The title applied rather to the style of the service and the pronunciation of the sacred language which, in Europe, often differed markedly from place to place. Later, with increased differentiation, the *shul* would be popularly named after specific towns, the Jassier, the Berdichever, the Odesser, the Krakauer, and so on. Every fresh contingent clung to the *nusach* (order of services) of its own locality. This condition, in one sense, was a source of strength. It enabled the immigrant, at landing, to savor the full flavor of his old religion. Indeed, in the smaller communities where there were no resources to indulge in the New York degree of differentiation, that element was often sadly missed.

But there were also disadvantages. While this insistence upon every jot and tittle of the old ways was touching evidence of the importance of religion in immigrant hearts, it created a chaotic organizational situation; and the chaos was further confounded by the shifts of population from neighborhood to neighborhood which left some edifices empty not long after they were built. The result was a looseness of structure and an absence of discipline that often led to intellectual and social confusion among the mass of Jews.

It was hard to define the relationship of each autonomous, free, and independent synagogue to the whole community. It was also hard, within any congregation, to locate a sovereign religious authority. In the old country, that role had been played by the rabbi, who was not primarily a preacher but the ecclesiastical head of the community and the judge on matters of ritual and law; his function was to study and interpret. Normally, worship in the synagogue proceeded without his assistance, and many American congregations likewise got by without the expense of maintaining a rabbi.

When the rabbi did appear on the scene, his authority and his role were not clearly defined, either in relation to the synagogue, of which he was a functionary, or to the Jewish community as a whole. The synagogue could hire and fire him at will, while the community was dominated by "secular organizations" and by individuals who were not necessarily members of any synagogue.

Because of this looseness of community structure, many functions, originally tied to the synagogue, fell into the hands of autonomous, disconnected new bodies. The earliest congregations had tried to make the *Kahal* what it had been in the Old World, the center of the whole life of their society. But once the synagogues multiplied in this disorganized fashion, no one of them, or group of them, could make a claim to universality. In addition, the impact of urban life tended to divide the allegiance of the individual immigrant. Not all the people who met to worship together in a given place were likely to be interested in the same activities or have the same point of view outside the place of worship. As the synagogue ceased to be comprehensive and general, as it became local and particular, many functions, not purely religious, fell into the hands of other local and particular institutions.

Three matters, above all, early aroused general concern. Among all immigrants there was a dread of dying alone, of isolation in the final moments of life on earth. The few who came together quickly made provision that they would give each other proper burial in the foreign soil on which they met. And for Jews, for whom this last human care had a religious significance connected with the hope for resurrection and for a future life, the cemetery ranked high in the list of communal needs. In the eighteenth century, and in the first half of the nineteenth, the cemetery was an adjunct of the synagogue. But increasingly, after the influx of immigrants in the 1840s, many who could not, or would not, affiliate permanently with a place of worship, still wished to be secure in this primary sense.

Almost as deep a source of concern was the possibility that illness, accident, or some other unforeseen disaster might deprive a man of his livelihood and his family of its support. Few of these people had found enough security in the United States to erect their own safeguards against such contingencies. Mostly they hoped for some organization that would do what, in the old country, the village had done spontaneously, and what, in early America, the synagogue had done informally.

Finally, there was a deep urge for company, for just the occasion to join with friends, to lose the sense of strangeness, and to maintain a measure of continuity with the life of the past.

To fill one, or a combination of several, of these needs, there sprang up a galaxy of organizations, large and small. Since they represented responses to the specific needs of specific people, these fell into no logical general pattern. Sometimes their purposes were confused. They overlapped each other in jurisdiction and membership, and very likely they were not efficiently managed. But they grew in numbers and in membership and held the loyalty of the immigrant; no one ever resigned from an organization unless it was to form a rival one.

Some had very narrow functions. There were *bikur cholim* societies, to visit the sick. There were *gemilath chasodim* societies which collected funds from which to make small loans to tide over those temporarily in distress.

Others assigned themselves a somewhat wider sphere. The

mutual benefit association was a voluntary group which accumulated monthly dues, and paid out stated benefits at death or illness, like an insurance company. Unlike the insurance company, however, these associations also assured consolation in illness, and mourners at funerals. In the beginning of the nineteenth century, Jewish immigrants seemed often to have joined the organizations of this kind set up by Germans without regard to sectarian affiliations, and in many places they continued to do so. But where Jews were numerous, the religious elements were important enough to lead early to the establishment of specifically Jewish groups; by 1847 there were two in New York, and the number grew without pause thereafter.

Most comprehensive of all was the lodge, increasingly popular with all Americans, which added to the burial, insurance, benefit, and fraternal functions, the embellishments of ceremony, ritual, and honorific titles. Some Jews were, and continued to be, prominent in the older American Masonic orders, while others joined the newer ones in which immigrants took a leading role, such as the Knights of Pythias and the Odd Fellows. Often in these general organizations there were local lodges in which Jews were a majority, or made up the whole membership.

Other Jews, however, formed orders distinctively their own, such as B'nai B'rith, founded in 1843, and the B'rith Abraham which quickly sprouted branches through the nation. At the outset, men were drawn to these orders through the hope of uniting Jews separated by religious and national differences. But each soon acquired a particular character, for their essential attraction was the comradeship of the like-minded.

Spontaneous or planned, these were the means by which immigrants protected themselves against the danger of being left alone in a foreign world. But these people, once settled, were moved also by the impulse to aid those who could not help themselves. No man among them was so well settled that he could not remember when, not far from want, he had himself been a stranger in the land. Charity, traditionally a religious virtue among Jews, here became a categorical obligation.

This too had once been within the orbit of the synagogue, but now it fell away into the hands of societies particularly charged with the function. Many congregations had customarily maintained funds from which the officers extended assistance to the resident and transient needy. Even later, the Jew in quest of alms could generally count on not being turned away empty-handed from the synagogue.

But the growth of population made it clear that these informal acts of generosity by synagogues and individuals were inefficient and ineffective. Some communities attempted to limit aid to "well-behaving" member families, when they "should, God forbid, be in need or trouble." Hard times, as in 1837, put a special strain on such resources. And good times or bad, the most deserving were too often overlooked, while the few gentry who made a fine thing of it, circulated from congregation to congregation. Furthermore, the Jewish poor were often immigrants, not known to the community, not members of any organization. In the 1840s and 1850s, in New York, Philadelphia, and other cities, Hebrew Benevolent Societies began to appear, their function to assure an equitable distribution of the community's aid.

The most important problems of aid were not those involved in getting the immigrants across the Atlantic. Indeed, it soon appeared that the first few years after entry were freest of trouble. The most trying difficulties seemed to come after two or three years of residence, when bodies were worn out with harsh and unaccustomed labor, when relatives felt they had already helped out enough, and when old social restraints wore thin from constant friction with the unfamiliar ways of urban living.

The first tentative steps toward ameliorating these conditions came at the middle of the nineteenth century. Hospitals seemed to have appeared first, lest the Jew faithful to his tradition be compelled to eat forbidden food, or face the danger of dissection after death. Cincinnati, New York, and Chicago in 1850, 1852, and 1868, led in building hospitals. In time, the larger communities also felt the obligation to support orphanages. Such institutions were set up in Philadelphia (1855), by B'nai B'rith in Cleveland (1868), and by the Hebrew Sheltering and Guardian Society in New York (1879). These homes, it was hoped, would prevent fatherless children from being "educated in such places where the greatest care is taken to imbue the youthful mind with sectarian and mystical doctrines." Despite the enormous cost of maintaining these agencies, they grew in number and in the quality of their services.

The philanthropic organizations, where they existed, had a deep effect upon the Jews who supported them. However, by so doing, these people did not cut themselves off from the rest of the world. As the Rev. J. J. Lyons of Shearith Israel pointed out in 1847, in an appeal for the victims of the Irish famine, the Jews were sensitive to their links with all humanity. But they were also conscious of distinctive needs as a group. They set up their own institutions at considerable cost instead of relying upon those public ones already available because they were aware of meaningful differences between themselves and other Americans. Conversely, the very existence of synagogues, societies, and charities, served to heighten and to perpetuate the consciousness of group identity.

In these activities, the size of settlement was often critical. Hospitals and orphanages, lodges and fraternal orders found support in cities with a substantial Jewish population. But the large number of Jews who, through these years, lived dispersed in smaller communities found no such resources to enrich their social life. The deficiency confronted them with a problem that was troubling to them personally, and more troubling still when they thought of their children.

The divergence of experience between small town and city was even more marked when it came to those societies which were essentially vehicles of culture. Every such organization bespoke the assumption that the members of the group had something unique to say to one another, that they shared, in some measure, a common heritage of ideas that were worth expressing and worth transmitting to their children.

In the larger cities, there were, by now, a considerable number of Jewish literary, dramatic, library, and musical societies. Some were specifically concerned with the Hebrew language, others with Jewish history and literature generally, and still others, like the Purim Associations, combined conviviality and culture. But these by no means fully absorbed the attention of the Jews who were also likely to join the more general associations in the community. In these matters, there was no essential competition; a German Jewish immigrant could, in good conscience, be a member of the Zion Literary Society, of the local turnverein or glee club, and of the Lyceum.

The vehicles of culture most difficult to bring into being were those that were highly institutionalized: schools, newspapers, and theaters. These were expensive to maintain, required a permanent organization, and were definite, visible signs of the separateness of the group in the total culture. They arose and persisted only in response to a clear-cut need.

Undoubtedly schools were the most important channels for transmitting ethnic ideas and culture from generation to generation. Yet the dominant conditions of American education were already set before the appearance of large groups of immigrants, and the newcomers were never in a position to revise the earlier decisions. By the 1840s it had been determined that the education of youth in the United States would be public, that is, governed by the state. Such training, it was clear, would also be almost entirely free and universal. From these premises, it followed as a matter of course that there would be no religious instruction in the public schools and that no public funds would go to religious schools. Although, in practice, sectarian control was not fully eliminated for several decades, the principle was firmly established and ultimately adhered to. As a result, any group that wanted full-time schools of its own had, out of its own resources, to compete with the public schools. Like the Catholics and Lutherans, Jews attempted to do so, but signally failed.

In the 1840s and 1850s a succession of day schools in Cincinnati, Chicago, Boston, Baltimore, and Philadelphia were added to a number of survivals from an earlier period. In New York, in 1847, two schools were in operation, and ten years later these offered instruction to more than eight hundred students. It is not likely that all these students were regular or full-time, although some at least followed an extensive curriculum that included study of the German language.

But it was soon obvious that such parochial institutions could not hold their own against the public schools. Like all those that would follow, they labored under serious handicaps. They were more expensive than many parents could afford. The best teachers found better careers elsewhere. Above all, these schools were not as likely to lead to social and economic advancement which depended on contacts outside the Jewish group. In this respect, attendance at a sectarian school was actually a liability rather than an asset.

In the decade after 1860, therefore, in the years when immigration had temporarily subsided, the attempts of these parochial schools to present a full curriculum petered out. The fact that Saturday classes were eliminated during this period in most public institutions, as was reading from dogmatic passages in the Bible, hastened the trend. It was characteristic that the Hebrew Free School Association of New York (1864) and the Jewish Educational Society of Chicago, both founded to resist the proselytizing of Christian missions, early confined their efforts to the children of the poor and made no attempt to parallel the course of studies in the public schools.

That the cultural activities of the American Jews were reflections of their conditions of settlement and not simply tra-

ditions carried over from the past or from abroad was also
shown in the emergence of new channels of expression. The
Jews who emigrated to the United States had not habitually
read newspapers at home; lack of interest and high cost had
made the appearance of a journal in the small towns of Germany or England something of a rarity. The same Jews, in
the New World, became regular, eager readers. The immigrant who bought a newspaper did so because it filled an
American need.

For many years, there were not enough Jews, even in the
largest American cities, to support Jewish newspapers. These
people had to find their news either in the American, English,
or the German press.

There were, however, a number of weeklies and monthlies
that combined the functions of newspapers and magazines.
These periodicals made no attempt to cover general news but
concentrated on the particular events that concerned their
group of readers, also giving space to discursive essays and
other "features." Some were primarily religious in interests;
others were linked to fraternal societies like B'nai B'rith. A
few appeared in German: *Zeichen der Zeit* (Chicago), *Israel's Herold* (New York), and *Deborah* (Cincinnati), for instance. But the more important ones used English as their medium, although they occasionally made the concession of introducing a German column. Among these were *The Occi-
dent* (Philadelphia), *The Jewish Messenger*, *The American
Hebrew*, *The Hebrew Leader* (all of New York), *The Israelite* (Cincinnati), *The Hebrew Observer*, *The Gleaner*, and
The Pacific Messenger (San Francisco). These journals penetrated places where no other news agencies existed. In the

semirural hamlets there was often an anxious wait at the post office. If the paper failed to come, it might be impossible to know the date of an approaching holiday or memorial anniversary. A tenuous tie but sometimes the only one, the weeklies held remote and lonely people in a distant attachment to a Jewish community.

For the most part, in other cultural affairs the Jews did not stand apart in this period. They were interested in the theater but saw neither opportunity nor need for separateness. Charles Dickson, Henry Dobbin, and other English Jews appeared in the earliest American dramas, and their German co-religionists played an important part in the theater that grew up among the German immigrants.

In the United States, the Jews stepped into a world different from that of Europe in its social structure and in its attitudes toward them. Nowhere else had they encountered the image Americans held of them. The new views compelled the Jews radically to revise their own conceptions of themselves and of the nature of their culture.

For one thing, the medieval background was absent. That difference in historical experience had certain general effects upon American society. It relieved this country of the stratified class structure and of the rigid social system that, in Europe, hampered movement from one level to another. Here, newcomers, Jews among them, were free to take whatever rank in society they could. More specifically, the difference in background meant that Jews were not weighed down by the survival of the medieval religious dogmas. On the contrary, the absence of an established church and the prevalence of latitudinarianism—the idea that, whatever its doctrines, any religion was good if it inculcated good morals—meant that the Jew stood in society, on a footing entirely equal with that of all other citizens.

Furthermore, the Jews carried into these years the accumulated favorable attitudes of the American past, attitudes that reached back to Puritan New England and the founding fathers. Not long before, John Adams had proclaimed them "the most glorious Nation that ever inhabited the Earth." The Jews, he asserted, had "influenced the affairs of Mankind more, and more happily than any other Nation ancient or modern."

Among the Jews, the numerous immigrants not infrequently met with rebuffs and slurs from the native-born. But it was the American ideal that men should be regarded in law as individuals and not as members of a group and that each should rise and fall on his own merits. This free atmosphere discouraged discrimination. Those Germans who, in Europe, were still moved by the old prejudices, seemed to shed the relics of the Old World in the course of becoming Americans. The contrast with the other side of the Atlantic was striking. In western Europe, emancipation was recent and incomplete; in the east, it did not exist at all.

Native Jews, even by 1820, had already come to terms with the new situation. In the next half-century, the newcomers discovered that part of the process of settlement was adjustment from the old conditions to the new.

In the fifty years after 1820 other Americans generally regarded Jewish immigrants as members of a nationality group, identified, like other nationality groups, largely by language.

They were thus uniformly considered Germans, one with other Germans who happened to be Lutherans or Catholics. This categorization, which lumped Poles, Czechs, Hungarians, and Hollanders together with the natives of the German states, was not surprising. Neither natives nor immigrants had ears sensitive enough to discriminate among all the shades of German dialect; furthermore, surviving examples reveal that the spoken German of Bavarian Jews in these years was not much closer to the language of Goethe than was the spoken Yiddish of Posner Jews.

The "Germans" (or, in Hebrew, *Ashkenazim*) did not immediately fuse with the native Jews any more than did German Catholic immigrants with native Catholics. In fact, the old American Jews, although actually descended from immigrants of many different nationalities, tried to disassociate themselves socially from the newcomers by stressing their own Sephardic (Spanish) background. Institutionally, that separation persisted for several decades.

Nor did the "Germans" fail to recognize divisions among themselves. The process of organizing synagogues showed how strong was the sense of locality. Little love was lost between the "Bayerische" and the "Hinter-Berliner"; they were free with criticism of one another's manners, dress, language, and piety. But still they were held together by a common social experience, by a common institutional life, and by fewness of numbers.

For, in this period, the percentage of Jews who ceased to affiliate with the Jewish community was rather large. The rate of intermarriage seems to have been substantial. Of course not every such union resulted in the loss of a member of the community; there is evidence that sometimes the children of such marriages remained within the fold. Nevertheless some loss by intermarriage was inevitable.

Other pressures also led to "leakage." Occasionally the Christian denominational journals carried accounts of Jewish conversions. But more often, the change was not that formal, not that noticed. Where settlements were sparse and scattered, isolated individuals and families simply lost contact and fell away. Often, the need for having a decent funeral, with some clergyman officiating, the need of finding a partner in marriage, was too great to be denied by loyalties worn thin in migration. As the second generation grew to maturity there was a strong likelihood that, eager to be Americanized, it would discard everything associated with the immigrant heritage of its fathers, including religion.

To the well-established native American Jews, this was no danger. Judaism was not "foreign" to their children as it was to the children of Germans and Poles. Some old Sephardic congregations, like Shearith Israel in New York and Mikveh Israel in Philadelphia, felt less compulsion to alter their ways radically, for they had gradually accommodated themselves to the attitudes of their American members. But the immigrants feared a split between the generations and, out of love for their children, attempted to hold them to the synagogue by Americanizing it in one fell swoop. If the synagogue did not adjust to the spirit of the age, said the *Israelite* in 1854, "we will have no Jews in this country in less than half a century."

This was the underlying popular motivation behind support of the reform movement. The first demands were for changes not in theology but in the externals of worship. There was a widespread desire for more respectability, the measure of respectability being the standards common to other Americans. Early in the century, Shearith Israel of New York introduced English into the service. For the same reasons, the cantors, or *hazonim*, began to assume for themselves the dignity of clergymen, after the Protestant sects. By the 1820s these men used the designation "Reverend," called themselves ministers or pastors, and were accustomed to appear in uniform clerical garb.

After 1840, as immigration and then dispersal mounted, the demand for such changes increased. There were calls for more decorum, for the omission of superfluous prayers that rendered services long and disorderly. There was a desire that the "Germanic and Slavonic dialects" yield to English and that the unseemly auctioning of honors cease. Some wished also for an end to the curtained women's gallery, the addition of an organ or mixed choir, of an English sermon as in other denominations. Later came complaints that the dietary laws were onerous, that attendance at the synagogue on Saturday was too difficult. Some congregations, like Emanu-El in New York and Har Sinai in Baltimore, introduced the new order all at once; others, like Rodeph Shalom and Keneseth Israel in Philadelphia, gradually. Sometimes there were disputes and secessions; sometimes the whole process of reform was quiet and orderly.

The desire to be like the other denominations also led the synagogues, reformed or not, to call rabbis to their service once they could afford to support them. With no American facilities for training a rabbinate, these clergymen had to be imported, generally from Germany. In part this was because a majority of the immigrants were themselves Germans, in part because Germany was then the center to which advanced Jewish thinkers and scholars came from all parts of Europe, and in part because German culture and learning then commanded the respect of all Americans, whether Jews or not.

The rabbis on arrival were decidedly a mixed lot, whether they were German, like Bernard Felsenthal, or non-German, like Marcus Jastrow. Max Lilienthal, educated in Munich, a hotbed of Jewish conservatism, was still orthodox when he came. Isaac M. Wise leaned toward the new ideas although he had not yet broken with the old. Samuel Hirsch, on the other hand, and David Einhorn already held reform tenets. But whatever their opinions, the critical element was the extent to which the American Jews desired the new departure. The rabbi followed the congregation, or left it, as Wise discovered in Albany and Lilienthal in New York.

The function of the rabbis was to formalize in theological terms the conception of Judaism toward which their congregations were groping. Wise and his contemporaries did so against a background of rationalism and ethics that were, in those years, also influencing the American Catholic and Protestant churches.

In the three decades after 1855 the new creed emerged. The Talmud was no longer considered a strict guide to practice, and Mosaic legislation was accepted only as a code of ethics. The reformers gave up the nationhood of the Jews and rejected such nationalistic holidays as Purim. In their view, the dispersion of the Jewish people was not a temporary punishment, preliminary to an eventual return to the Land of Israel, but a permanent, providential condition. The mission of the Jews was to "lead the nations to the true knowledge and worship of God," and they were allied thus to Christianity and Islam in the struggle for common social ideals.

This position was so close to that of the Liberal Christianity of the mid-nineteenth century that Rabbi Sarner, in an examination by an army board of chaplains, could be mistaken for a Lutheran! Yet the position of the reformers by no means involved a rejection of Judaism; it was more properly an effort to stem the tide of conversion. Indeed, the *Jewish Chronicle*, organ of the Christian missionaries seeking to convert the Jews, recognized that when it directed its most explosive salvos, not at the orthodox, but at the "modernized reform infidels." If the pews and pulpit and whole interior of the synagogue increasingly took on the appearance of the church, there was still a desire, manifest in Moorish and Byzantine exteriors, to preserve a visible connection with the Jewish past. This was Judaism Americanized according to the way of the times.

The momentous half-century that ended in 1870 had thus not altogether broken with the past. Certainly immigration had altered the Jewish community, just as expansion had altered the nation to which they had come. Nonetheless an underlying continuity was still there, as these Americans, remaining Jews, stimulated by the challenges of liberty in American society, began to explore the deeper meaning of their faith.

CHAPTER FIVE

The Flight from Eastern Europe

After a long uneasy preparation, the destruction of east European society began, after 1870, to move toward its frightening climax. An old order, in this half of the continent, had not the resilience to meet the successive blows that beat upon it from the west. Improved communications had shrunk the middle distances in the nineteenth century, and without a protective margin of space, the old regimes of squires and peasants, of priests, of guilds, of ruthless order, could not stand up against the insidiously infiltrating new productive techniques, new ideas, and new social relationships. Tottering after mid-century, eastern Europe proceeded toward the disintegration that war and revolution would complete after 1914.

The Jews had been part of this society. Its disasters overwhelmed them. The concentration of landholding and the growth of large-scale agriculture that squeezed out the peasants also eliminated the function of the Jews as middlemen. The rise of manufacturing destroyed the independence of the artisan and reduced him to a wage-earning factory worker. A few Jews in the growing cities found or made new places, or sometimes fortunes, in the constant reshuffling of opportunities. But the masses in the villages saw their way to a livelihood become narrower and more difficult year by year.

Meanwhile, the number to be accommodated grew ever larger. The incessant rise of population created a growing pool of young men with nothing to do, men who lived on dreams and mournfully hopped from one expedient to another, desperately buying and selling to earn the watery gruel of their subsistence. By 1900, in Galicia, where the situation was extreme, there was a Jewish trader trying to scratch a living out of every ten peasants, and the average value of the stocks of these merchants came to some twenty dollars. Clearly there was no room for these people; most of them would have to seek their living in some other fashion. More often now their eyes turned westward. The revolutions that had destroyed the economic position of millions of other European artisans and peasants also forced the Jews to move.

Other tragic events, however, increased the attractiveness of the golden land beyond the sea, and made the risks of migration less frightening. Pogroms, products of peasant unrest and government encouragement, in 1870, 1881, 1899, and 1905, hurried Jews away from Romania and Russia. Cholera and famine, as in 1869, had the same effect. And, in the Czar's domains, persecution, compulsory military service, and the confinement of Jews to the Pale of Settlement had a similar outcome. The Jews in Russia, forbidden by law to cross east of the constricting pale or boundary, huddled together in Lithuania, Poland, and the Ukraine, could not move to Moscow as easily as the Jews in Prussia to Berlin, and therefore were more likely to leave the country altogether.

Persecution alone drove no one away; the bitter policy of the Hapsburgs in Galicia in the first half of the nineteenth century created no exiles. On the other hand, when the volume of emigration increased after 1870, it was as high in Austria-Hungary, where there were no pogroms and where government policy was by then relatively liberal, as in Russia where the reverse was true. But the persecutions were significant to the degree that they persuaded Jews they were not at home where they were and, with economic opportunity lost, had better turn to migration.

The influence of the enlightenment was analogous. Subtly, knowledge of the wider world had crept into the stifling villages. Secular books, bearers of new facts, new ideas, new visions, had broken through the closed circle of the old study halls and left the young men with new hopes. There were alternatives to the endlessly repetitive life of poverty and persecution they now led. The alternatives lay many miles distant, but the road lay open and they had only to follow it.

In ever growing numbers they moved—some openly under the eyes of officials glad to be quit of them, and some by stealth through the woods across the border; some by cart and some by foot and some by the hurtling railroad cars that now reached across the continent. The earliest ones wandered their own way from town to town to the seaports. The later ones had the aid of their predecessors and of philanthropic organizations, as well as the lore accumulated from the letters of those who had gone ahead: what it was like in Jassy or Hamburg or Liverpool; how one lived in the steerage of a steamship; and what one said to successive examining officials.

The movement grew steadily larger, as the conditions that had produced it grew worse. In the climactic outburst of the nine years before World War I, one and a quarter million Jews, one-seventh of all those in Europe, left it.

Great numbers took the same road as other displaced Europeans and came to America. For those who made the total break, there were, from time to time, alternatives—western Europe, England, South America, South Africa. Palestine attracted Zionists and, earlier, the participants in the *Bilu* movement. But through the nineteenth and twentieth centuries the United States consistently was the destination of the largest number. For most Jews on the move, the land of opportunity was across the Atlantic. In that respect, they were like all other peoples in the stream of immigration away from Europe. The curve of Jewish immigration to the United States runs remarkably parallel to that of general immigration to America, an indication that the decisive forces were the general ones common to the whole movement.

After 1870 Jewish immigration bore overwhelmingly east European qualities. Germans continued to come of course, but as the nineteenth century drew to a close, their numbers were far smaller than those from central and Russian Europe. Furthermore, the development of railway and steamship lines which sold through-tickets, good from the point of origin to the final destination, eliminated the occasion for an intermediate German experience for transients; travelers less frequently found themselves stranded by exhausted funds.

Finally, the disruptive influences of emancipation were so completely diffused now that men at every level of society understood the inevitability of a break with the past. Formerly, only the *maskilim*, intellectuals influenced by German thought, had thought a new departure necessary in Jewish life. Thus Michael Heilprin, back in the 1850s had moved from Poland, by way of Hungary, to America, there to become editor of *Appleton's New American Cyclopaedia* and *The Nation*. But three decades later, even the most orthodox were aware that conditions could only deteriorate further where they were, that it was necessary to migrate.

These latter years of the nineteenth century were different in orientation in another sense. The Jews had been a minority among the emigrants from Germany, far outnumbered by non-Jewish artisans and traders. But in eastern Europe the Jews were almost alone as emigrants, and were first to take the move; in Galicia, for instance, where Jews were only 12 per cent of the population, they supplied 60 per cent of the immigrants between 1881 and 1890. Peasants from that part of the continent later came in large numbers, but not until after 1890. The fact that these Jews arrived first of their conationals would significantly influence the course of their Americanization.

The numbers involved in this period of Jewish immigration were also much larger than before 1870. In the single year, 1906, over 150,000 arrived in the United States, more than came in any decade before the Civil War. In the years between 1870 and 1914, the entries mounted up to more than two million, of whom more than 60 per cent originated in Russia, and more than 20 per cent in Austria-Hungary.

Outside the main stream of Jewish immigration from Europe were a number of supplementary currents that added nearly fifty thousand "Oriental" Jews. Natives of Greece and Turkey, Syria and Morocco, their languages Greek, Arabic, and Ladino, they joined in the New World other Jews with whom they had had little contact for some five hundred years.

World War I caused an interruption which allowed less than a hundred thousand Jews to reach America in the course of the conflict. But the tide of Jewish immigration seemed about to resume when a quarter-million crossed the Atlantic in the four years after 1920. Then, suddenly, the whole movement was choked off by a reversal of the traditional American attitude toward immigration in general.

A growing fear of foreigners, stimulated by the nationalistic passions of the war years led, between 1920 and 1924, to the enactment of legislation which curtailed the number of entrants drastically. What was more, the limitation was imposed in terms of a quota system, based on nativity, that excluded almost all south and east Europeans, among whom were the great bulk of prospective Jewish immigrants.

In 1927 a new law further reduced the number for whom the gates remained open, and in 1930, an executive order effectively stopped up the remaining chinks in the wall around the promised land. Although there were occasional relaxations in individual cases, the barriers in general were insurmountable. A whole epoch in American history had come to a close.

By then the American Jewish population was formed. The total had grown to almost four million in 1917 and to more than four and a quarter million in 1927—immigrants and children of immigrants, whom war and persecution and, most of all, the fundamental economic dislocation of modern times had summoned to a new life in a new world.

After 1870 the immigrants reached a new America. Agricultural production was still expanding and the last open stretches of the great plains were filling up with settlers. But the economic energies of the country were now primarily devoted to manufacturing. Aggressive exploitation drew upon the rich mineral resources of the continent for the raw materials: coal and iron, copper and lead, and millions of barrels of petroleum for light and power. In scores of mills, heavy industry turned these into useful products of iron and steel: rails and bridges, agricultural implements and automobiles, and machines of countless shapes and functions. And in thousands of other factories, those machines were set to work to make the goods for swelling home and foreign markets.

Now the American frontier was in the cities. Here the mammoth factories arose, hives to which the workers swarmed daily. Here the lines of transport led, along which goods came to be exchanged and transformed. Here were the centers of distribution and of financial control. Although the city had always had a place in American life and had grown steadily from the start, it now entered upon its period of critical significance and greatest growth.

After 1870 the conditions of industrial development and urban life would determine the adjustment of all immigrants, and most of all of the Jews. These newcomers would not be able to disperse themselves as their predecessors had. Their difficulties and their opportunities alike would lie in other directions.

It was not surprising in view of their past, that some Jews coming off the boat still thought of their future life as one of trade. As earlier, the easy access to commerce was through peddling. If there was a relative to stake him, the ambitious young man could be out with a basket the next morning; if not, he would learn before long where the wholesalers were who would advance him goods on credit. Then he was out, following the unknown roads to his future. Shouldering his *pak tsores*, his bag of woes, he wandered into strange districts, edging into trolley cars, braving the taunts and stones of boys and their elders, avoiding the signs "No Beggars or Peddlers Allowed."

It was not as easy as it had been earlier in the century to find a happy end to such a road. Too many places were already preempted. Farm women, more settled, had established buying habits, traveling more frequently to town to do their shopping or relying upon the mail-order catalogue. In the cities, the growth of retailing and of one-price chain and department stores, further limited the peddler's sphere of operations. He became mostly a hawker of odds and ends, serving the marginal groups of immigrants and others unfamiliar with the new American buying patterns. Some found it still possible, by labor, frugality, and calculation to accumulate from peddling a little store of capital. Only it took more labor, more frugality, and more calculation than formerly.

The young fellows were likely to chose an easier way into business. If they had acquired a command of English and a fairly good hand at writing, they often preferred to do their traveling for wholesalers. After the Civil War, the tribe of drummers increased rapidly, establishing a network of distribution by which shopkeepers in the remotest hamlets were brought into contact with the great urban markets. The Jewish drummer became a familiar figure, nattily dressed, blowing in and out of town with a style. In 1880 George H. Jessop's play *Sam'l of Posen* made him a popular hero who exposes the villain and earns from a grateful patron "a start in business."

The hardships of peddling and the uncertainties of the life of the traveling salesman increased the attractiveness of more settled lines of business. Generally, the itinerant merchants waited only long enough to scrape together the cash for the first month's rent and for a modest stock, before they were standing behind their own counters. Although the virgin opportunities in the field were gone after 1870, and ever greater sums of capital were required for a start, the possibility of success still existed, even for those who began with humble resources.

The way from pushcart in the ghetto market to chromium and plate glass on Main Street remained open as long as the economy expanded. The newcoming Jews joined many more of their native brethren in petty retailing. They became grocers, stationers, and confectioners, and dealers in dry goods and clothing. Some came quickly to the dead ends of bankruptcy and failure. But the majority ran their businesses at a modest level, earning a decent livelihood for themselves, and saving to make the way easier for their children. A few, generally the native-born, built their businesses into substantial enterprises. They catered to a growing middle class who were developing their tastes for consumers' goods but had not yet the means to supply their wants by custom orders. The wives of clerks and doctors were eager to keep abreast of fashion in their clothes and in the furnishings of their homes but yet were content to have their gowns and sofas made by machines, standardized after a pattern in a factory. Furthermore, in the great cities, such purchasers were incapable of seeking out the particular shops that could serve them best; they preferred to deal in a large store which would gather together the diverse articles they needed and would be reliable as to price and quality.

In the development of the department store, Jews played a prominent part. Isador Straus had been a clerk in his father's store in the small Georgia town of Talbotton. As a young man, he began to trade in cotton on his own account and accumulated a little capital. By 1874 he was established in New York, dealing in glassware and dishes. That year he acquired the concession of the crockery department in R. H. Macy and Company, an overgrown dry-goods store like Stewart's, Wanamaker's, Jordan's, and others through the country that were about to make the transition to the new form. Before long he became a partner and, joined by his brother, converted Macy's into the world's largest department store. So, too, Adam Gimbel's seven sons left Vincennes, Indiana, for the opportunities of merchandising in the big city; and Altman and Bloomingdale, Halle and Lazarus, Stix and Filene became significant names in the evolution of American retailing.

In the same years the son of German Jewish immigrants was applying the same principles to the mail-order business and making Sears Roebuck a byword in countless homes. Born in Springfield, Illinois, Julius Rosenwald had come roundabout to Chicago by way of New York, where he had served his apprenticeship in trade. In 1893 he was manufacturing clothing when he became interested in Sears, a house that had been selling watches and jewelry by mail and was now branching out in other lines. Rosenwald invested in the business, broadened its operations, and in little more than a decade had brought its annual sales up to fifty million dollars.

Whether in the polished office of the department store or

behind the counter of the corner grocery, retailing was perhaps the most satisfactory means of economic adjustment: it
involved hard work and, at most levels, insecurity, but it enabled the Jew to adjust gently to his new situation in life. In
the store he had the boss's sense of independence; he had the
dignity of a man who could take time off to observe the Sabbath; and he had the comfort of preserving the family structure, for in these enterprises the whole family worked together.

Retail trade had many ramifications. Some who started in
such businesses occasionally extended their activities to other
phases of distribution. There were abundant new opportunities in wholesaling, in jobbing, and in brokerage. Dealers in
secondhand goods were likely to become auctioneers and to
undertake the handling of waste products, and many, on the
side, invested in real estate. The same process was also the
means for entering manufacturing, notably in the clothing,
cigar, and furniture industries where fabrication first developed
as an adjunct of distribution. But these fields were only the
points of largest concentration. In the rapid expansion of new
industry after 1870, enterprising and hard-working Jews built
up thriving companies in many other spheres as well. Ferdi-
nand Sulzberger and the Morris family in meat packing, the
Guggenheims in mining, and the Cones in textiles showed the
variety of available opportunities.

By contrast, merchants of the type of Lopez and Touro disappeared. To some extent their function was carried on into
the twentieth century by the great banking families Seligman,
Schiff, Loeb, Lehman, and Warburg who helped recruit overseas capital for investment in the United States. But more generally the Jewish involvement in international trade declined

as commerce became less personal and less dependent on family connections and more institutionalized and routined.

The nature of the more striking economic contributions of some individuals must not obscure the fact that for the majority of Jews, and particularly for the great mass of immigrants, the way to a livelihood was beset with persistent difficulties. Increasingly the course of American economic development drove these people to work in the ranks of industry.

Every manufacturer now found his new factories dependent upon the unskilled immigrant labor that manned his machines, and that labor force, by its very availability, made possible the phenomenal growth of industry. In the last two decades of the nineteenth century there emerged, for the first time in the United States, an extensive Jewish proletariat to take its place beside the Irish, German, English, and native laborers. Earlier a number of artisans had transplanted their skills from the Old World to the New. But the wage-earning unskilled worker was a stranger to American Jewry until well after the Civil War.

This development was a product of the increased rate of immigration. The enormous numbers, rising steadily after 1870, could be absorbed in no other way. Moreover, the condition of their arrival and the port of debarkation itself encouraged the tendency to take employment in factories. In those years a noticeable concentration in shipping routes and shipping lines brought an ever-larger proportion of Jewish newcomers to the single port of New York. And these people were less able to break away from the place in which they landed. At the turn of the century, the immigrant brought with him an average of only eight dollars a head and faced the immediate necessity of finding work to keep himself and his family alive.

Like the Irish and other earlier immigrants in a similar position, the Jews turned to the rapidly expanding garment trades. The production of every article of apparel was now shifting from the consumer's own home, or the shop of the custom seamstress and tailor, to the factory and the machine. Men's coats and ladies' cloaks, shirts and blouses, hats and caps, fur mantles and silk ties, boned corsets and laced chemises—all these garments now became cheaply mass produced. The value of products in the ready-made women's clothing industry rose by 133 per cent in the decade 1890–1900 alone.

The Jews became involved in the garment industries not by virtue of any inherent proclivity for the needle or because of previous training but because here was a constant demand for cheap labor. Most of these were "Columbus tailors" wedded to the "Katrinka" (the sewing machine) after they reached the land of Columbus.

Some Jews were already active in the clothing industries as manufacturers and were able to take on large numbers of immigrants as workers. In New York, in Philadelphia, in Boston, in Rochester, and, to a lesser degree, in Chicago, thousands of Jews found at the end of their long journey, the shears, the iron, and the treadle of the sewing machine. Bound thereafter to those tools, they toiled to clothe a nation. By 1890 well over thirteen thousand were so employed on the East Side of New York alone, and for two decades more their numbers grew steadily, as one *landsman* (fellow countryman) taught another, as relatives introduced their "greener" to the same occupations.

Low wages were characteristic of the industry; for that matter, they were characteristic of all branches of manufacturing that employed unskilled labor. Still, the harsh fact was that before 1910 a man's work in the garment trades was not likely to bring him more than twelve dollars a week, when he worked. And what of the long periods when he did not work, the slack seasons, the weeks of unemployment? It was an inescapable condition of the new life that the earnings of a single breadwinner could not be depended upon to keep a household going. The women had to work, and the children too.

This circumstance made it somewhat easier for the immigrant to accept the ignominies of homework and the sweating system, by which the laborers performed one process at home on a piecework basis. Since, in any case, all the family's hands had to serve, it was better that they should work together as a unit with their own kind under circumstances that made it possible for them to observe the Sabbath. In the crowded tenement quarters, dimly lighted whether by sun or lamp, the yards of cloth mounted up in heaps, waiting for tired fingers to transform them into the New World's fashions.

By the abstract measurements of health and sanitation this was worse than the factory. But the laborers had no choice. Increasingly, factory owners relied upon outside contractors and kept in the workshop only the very skilled tasks, like cutting, beyond the reach of most immigrants. The manufacturer could thus divorce himself from responsibility for the conditions under which garments were made in the tenements. He could also squeeze the competing contractors who, in turn, squeezed the too-eager workers a little more. The employees knew soon enough that the boss steadily manipulated piecework rates to lower their returns. No better than the inspectors did they like the filth in which they lived and slaved. They felt the hunger, the tiredness, the shame of it all more keenly than any social investigator. But they were trapped.

Or, almost trapped. Toiling as they did in the tenement, at home or near the home, they clung to the illusion of independence. Their working day was long, it was true. But perhaps if they worked a little harder they could finally break through the darkness into the golden land of dreams. And surely enough, for some, behind the illusion was a shred of reality. Often enough to keep hope alive, the more fortunate were able to throw off their wage-earning status and become "businessmen." Not the pressers indeed, for these, by common reputation, were uniformly a dull lot. But the ambitious cloak-maker could aspire to edge in as a contractor in the highly morcellized organization of the industry.

Although some labored days without end at the same trade, others succeeded in becoming employers or in leaving the industry altogether. After 1900 a larger proportion of the unskilled tasks fell to the lot of still newer immigrants, Poles and Bohemians in Chicago, Italians in New York, Armenians in Boston. And the trend became more pronounced after World War I.

Although the largest number of Jewish laborers were lumped together in this single field of manufacturing, there were enough seekers after jobs to find places in other pursuits as well. Jews found work in a great variety of manual employment, sometimes because of the special skills they had brought with them but more often through the accidents of acquaintanceship that revealed an opening or offered an entree to a trade. Some rolled cigars, at home or in shops. Some labored in the building industry, for wages if they had to, or preferably for hire, as independent painters, glaziers, and carpenters. Still others found their living in the printing trades, in the fabrication of jewelry, in the amusement business, and in a wide variety of jobs as clerks and salespeople. Indeed, Jews were employed almost everywhere, except in heavy manufacturing, in mining, and in agriculture.

There were determined but largely unsuccessful efforts to induce Jews to take up farming as a way of life. The plans of Noah and others for large-scale resettlement were not forgotten after the Civil War. When Jacob Schiff and Michael Heilprin, in the 1880s, suggested that agriculture was the solution to the immigrants' problems, they were only following long precedent, in accord with the prevailing American conception of a good life and in accord with the Jews' own aspirations.

Not a few idealistic young people, particularly in Russian cities like Kiev and Odessa, dissatisfied with the kind of lives their folk had led in the Old World, came to the United States with the firm intention of becoming more productive, of getting closer to the soil. In 1882 several groups of the organization *Am Olam* came to America and pitched agricultural settlements at Sicily Island, Louisiana; Crémieux, South Dakota; and New Odessa, Oregon. In a major effort that year, the Hebrew Immigrants' Aid Society also settled several hundred families in Catopaxi, Colorado, and in the towns of Alliance, Carmel, and Rosenhayn, New Jersey. The Baron de Hirsch Fund in 1891 founded the colony of Woodbine, also in New Jersey, and the same agency stood ready to make loans and to give advice to any would-be farmers. Meanwhile, the Jewish Colonization Association actively planned settlements that would enable organized groups of immigrants to make agricultural careers for themselves. The Yiddish press regularly added its encouragement. Lest traditional prejudices stand in the way, the *Morning Journal* in 1914 pointed out that the American farmers "are similar to the small noblemen of our old home rather than to the degraded and oppressed peasants."

The sum total of all these efforts was remarkably slim; by 1912 there were less than four thousand Jewish families on the land. Whatever allowances must be made for poorly chosen sites, and for the unforeseen calamities of nature, the fact remains that Jewish immigrants were not tempted by the realities of being "small noblemen." The intellectuals were quickly discouraged, and the others usually failed to make a living. Despite the fact that subsidized industries were brought in to furnish supplementary income, the colonies in New Jersey fell off dishearteningly; the three hundred families there in 1882 were only two hundred ten years later, and only seventy-six in 1896. Where the effort took root and flourished, it was in specialized forms of commercial agriculture—dairying with which some immigrants had had experience in the old country, poultry raising, and summer-boarder farming. These activities were carried on in the vicinity of the big cities, and therefore, New Jersey, lower New York, and New England held all but a few of the Jewish husbandmen.

The failure of these efforts was revealing. There was no aversion to the land; Jews on the contrary tended to over-idealize it. But positive cultural and economic factors stood in the way. Apart from very general discouragements of isolation and loneliness and, outside the colonies, the difficulties of orthodox observance, Jewish immigrants found this form of life unsatisfactory.

Agriculture, in this period, lacked the compensation trade offered, a *tachlis*, a purpose worth striving for. The crucial test was that the children were discontent and eager to be off, wanting to be trained either for the technical and scientific aspects of farming or for the general opportunities of the city. Nor was that trend surprising in a period when the children of native American farmers were also deserting the family homesteads for the attractions of the towns, when the percentage of economically active Americans in agriculture fell from 50 per cent in 1870 to 20 per cent in 1940.

In part, the seeming absence of opportunity also accounts for the unwillingness of Jewish immigrants to enter heavy industry. Not that long days and nights at labor in the service of the sewing machine, or the drudgery of candy or grocery store were any easier. But the few guided to the steel mill, railroad, or mine saw no purpose in hand-to-mouth living, no prospect of improving their own status or that of their children, of becoming a real American boss. "A Russian student," recorded a social worker, "beat his way to Cincinnati from the mines, on a freight train. Eating nothing for two days but coffee grains which he found in the box car, he was almost famished. One year later he was part owner in the hot tamale trust."

The promises of the New World consisted, in their view, not of drudgery at the machines in factory or field. To the extent that they could exercise choices, they devoted their energies where hope lay.

For that reason, although relatively few attained the goal, the professions held for Jews a constant allure. The enormous expansion of such occupations after 1890 seized their imaginations. To the degree that doctors and dentists, teachers and lawyers were more often trained in schools than by apprenticeship, and more often appointed by examination than by favor, these professions became free, that is, open to ability rather than to personal or family contacts. Here, indeed, was a purpose worth slaving for. To some immigrants the goal seemed close enough to be reached personally; by 1905 there were almost five hundred Russian Jewish doctors in New York City alone. Many more transferred their hopes to the next generation, and toiled in the exciting faith they were opening doors for their children.

As the twentieth century advanced the number of Jews who enriched American life through such pursuits grew rapidly. In the second decade, Louis D. Brandeis was appointed to the Supreme Court of the United States, and Benjamin N. Cardozo and Felix Frankfurter, who would later also take places on that bench, had already entered upon distinguished careers. In medicine there were striking achievements by Abraham Jacobi in pediatrics, by Marion B. Sulzberger in dermatology, and by Isaac Levin in the treatment of cancer. A. A. Michelson made noteworthy contributions to physics. Among the philosophers of eminence were Felix Adler and Morris R. Cohen; among the social scientists, I. A. Hourwitch, E. R. A. Seligman, Edward Sapir, Franz Boas, and Charles Gross; and among the journalists, Joseph Pulitzer, Adolph S. Ochs, and Walter Lippmann.

No doubt these famous men were remote from the mass of

Jews who labored in the sweatshops or who waited on trade. Yet these distinguished few helped set the goals toward which the millions strived. The vision of a son's becoming a doctor or a lawyer kept many a man patiently at the needle and blotted out the dismal sight of the environment in which he passed his days.

Most Jews, like almost all other Americans in these years, faced the necessity of adjusting to one very fundamental change. If they were natives, they had very likely been born and lived their youth in the little towns of the rustic country-side. If they were immigrants, they had left behind them tiny villages, places where even a ghetto was not cut off from the open fields. Now before them were the narrow passages of the great cities, stoned in from the sight of nature, and crammed to overbursting with people and man-made objects. Only those who had had an earlier experience in one of the European or American urban centers were prepared for the newness of this life. Most had snatched only passing glimpses of the great places as they changed trains or as they moved through the seaports, London or Liverpool, Hamburg or Bremen.

Yet an ever-larger proportion of the Jews in the United States were destined to spend their days in the great American metropolitan regions. After 1890 about two-thirds of the Jews in America would consistently reside in the four largest cities, New York, Chicago, Philadelphia, and Boston. In that period, the first-named alone embraced about one-half of the total. This concentration was, in part, due to the fact that these places were then attracting all manner of young men, Jew and Gentile alike, from the interior of the country. In part, also, the concentrations in these cities sprang from their relationship to immigration.

The transatlantic shipping lines now tended to converge upon the port of the Hudson. Given the circumstances of their coming, roughly three-fourths of the Jews who landed at Castle Garden or Ellis Island perforce stayed in New York, stayed where they could immediately and most profitably dispose of their labor, get higher wages, and live at lower costs.

From this massive accumulation of souls, New York developed its uniqueness in American-Jewish life. Here was scope enough for the emergence of the whole range of communal institutions and activities; in this vast body were enough resources to support synagogues and charities, newspapers and schools, theaters and societies. In turn, these institutions made New York the focal point of Jewish group life in the whole nation. From this profusion of organizations and publications, there radiated an influence that, to some degree, affected the Jews in the farthest corners of the land. And, in addition, who in America did not have some contact, or the memory of a contact, with the Knickerbocker metropolis? Everyone passed through at one time or another and had at least a cousin living there.

In respect to the fullness of social and institutional life, the other cities ranged downward from New York according to the size of their Jewish population. The Philadelphia community, boasting a long history, had once been the largest in the United States, and grew rapidly with continued immigration. Boston and Chicago had a more recent Jewish development; large-scale settlement did not come until after 1840, but then multiplied quickly. By 1940 these cities and their environs each numbered two hundred thousand Jews or more.

In all these places there was a high proportion of wage earners among the immigrants for whom the adjustment to urban living involved particularly grave problems. The cities, half-formed and in any case suffering from extreme growing pains, could not absorb so many newcomers, especially impecunious ones. How could the resources of housing expand fast enough to shelter the seven million extra bodies that were added to New York and Chicago alone in the fifty years after 1870! With the demand so great, the Jews, like other immigrants, for many years were compelled to get by with unhappy makeshifts.

In each of the great cities was an area of primary settlement, the lower East Side in New York, the West Side in Chicago, the North End in Boston, downtown in Philadelphia. Here each successive wave of newcomers had found accommodations of a sort. Here low-rental quarters were available to Jews as the Irish and Germans, who had formerly lived there, improved their position and moved away.

Density of population was the most striking characteristic of these regions. On the East Side of New York, in 1916, were fully 700,000 Jews, to say nothing of Italians, Irishmen, and other folks. Naturally, land was at a premium. In New York and Boston the high value of every square foot led to the erection of tenement houses, towering six- or eight-story structures which utilized every inch so cunningly that twenty-four to forty families, one hundred to three hundred people, could find homes in a plot 20 by 100 feet. In Philadelphia and Chicago, cities not so completely hemmed in by water, there was more room in which to spread out and the tall tenement was not so common. Instead, there was a tendency to convert old frame houses and warehouses, to put one building in the yard of another, and to indent the blocks with blind alleys in the process of exploiting unused space.

Whatever the variations, all such quarters were characterized by a common poverty and by miserable sanitary conditions. Conveniences that were not known in the old country were not "missed." But here, the consequences of not having them were disastrous. In the narrow, crowded rooms, dirt crept up on the family, despite the unavailing efforts of the housewife, oppressed with so many other unfamiliar tasks. In the winter a bitter cold swept into the unheated flats and brought suffering that was matched only by the effects of the stinking heat of summer.

It was a hard life, yet most survived it. The death rate for Jews in these districts was not higher than that for comparable age groups living under better conditions. Tuberculosis was less common than among other immigrants, although as the slums took their toll, the Jewish rate began to rise steadily until the 1920s. Physically, the most pronounced effect seemed to be an inclination toward nervous diseases, perhaps a consequence of the unending struggle against insecurity. Yet there was no tendency toward drunkenness; at most, there was a kind of characteristic addiction to tobacco and to gambling. They were poor people and, inevitably, there were some paupers among them. They lived hemmed in by violence and produced a few gangsters, but not so many as to disturb the whole body; criminality rates by and large were low.

What seems to have furnished a saving balance was the fact

that family life was sound enough to preserve an element of stability and cultural health. There were shocks in plenty to rock the family: the lack of space; the obligation of women and children to work; the presence of boarders who helped make up the rent but also consumed valuable space; and the husbands here and there, discouraged and discontent, despairing of ever being able to cope with these bitter obligations, who went out on an errand and never returned. Though for a time the desertion problem was a serious one, the percentage remained small. These people generally came in family units and clung together; if the wife was a *tsore* (affliction), children were always a blessing. And with that bastion of security, the American ghetto was tolerable; in fact, it even had its compensations.

Here a man was not so much alone among strangers but rather was safe among his own kind. The tenement was close to work, a factor which saved precious carfare. And here were all the familiar institutions that eased the adjustment to new conditions, the synagogue and ritual bath, the Jewish theater and the kosher butcher. Certainly for the women it was easier to shop on Hester or Maxwell streets than to risk contacts with foreign ways and foreign goods.

For the immigrant, then, the area of primary settlement was often tolerable, but he soon learned that it was not of himself alone he had to think. On his children, particularly on those born in America, the effect of such life was harsh. Scornful of the discipline of the school, with parental authority weakened by the stigma of foreignness, driven into the streets because there was no room in the home, boys and girls grew up wild. Too young they went off to work, as newsboys or in shops, and who could tell what influences played upon them? The rate of juvenile delinquency was high, and even parents who did not read the cold statistics knew their children were pagans, in danger of being lost. Then, too, was this a place from which to marry off a daughter?

As the American generation grew up, the immigrant parents thought of moving. If they did not think of it, the children called it to their attention. They did not flee the ghetto. Far from it; they rather sought a superior place to which they could take the ghetto with them. First they moved to a contiguous area, say across the bridge to Williamsburg or over to Harlem, or to the other side of Boston and Chicago, the West End and South Side. Then, if there were resources enough, they became interested in something better; they looked for space and fresh air, and the sight of a bit of green. Only now they must move farther out, avoiding the intermediate settlements of other ethnic groups. But trolley lines and subways carried them out to Brownsville and the Bronx, Dorchester and Chelsea, and with them, *shul* and candy store. Here one could live in a two-family house or a triple-decker, join a land association, and perhaps become a landlord, perhaps have the luxury of a yard—for a while, that is. For, a whole army followed the first comers; the suburb too filled up and there were further extensions, in Borough Park and Flatbush, Brookline and Lawndale. By 1926 the number of Jews in the East Side of New York had fallen from the 700,-000 of 1916 to 500,000.

In the nice districts there was usually but a cold welcome for those who came so eagerly. The pervasive dread of crowding, associated with the fear of lowered standards and status, created deep resentment of any strangers. The earlier comers, having worked to escape the city, disliked its catching up with them in the persons of the Jews and other immigrants escaping from the slums. Often that resentment existed although the earlier comers were themselves Jews, native-born and prosperous and unwilling to be degraded by identification with the newcomers. The rebuffs and slights, real and fancied, that developed in the course of the outward movement of settlement contributed substantially to the bitterness between "German" and "Russian" Jews in these years.

If the leaders of the Jewish communities of 1900 could have looked ahead a quarter-century, they would nevertheless have judged this spreading out to be good. For in the early days, as population accumulated in New York and Philadelphia, there was a vivid fear that the consequences might be socially, physically, and economically disastrous. Already in 1850 New York philanthropists were planning to shift a "surplus" of population to Illinois. In the 1880s the United Hebrew Charities spent a good deal of energy encouraging removals, and after 1890 a national committee for ameliorating the conditions of the Russian refugees labored to distribute the newcomers throughout the country.

By 1900, with the trend toward concentration unabated, there was positive terror at the degrading conditions of the ghetto. The report of the United Hebrew Charities of New York City that year cried out for relief, and partly in response, B'nai B'rith embarked upon a program of spreading the new arrivals into the interior. In 1901 the effort was formalized with the establishment of the Industrial Removal Office, with branches in Philadelphia and Boston, and aided by the Baron de Hirsch Fund. Five years later came still another project: with the influential backing of Jacob Schiff there was an attempt to divert immigrant shipping to the port of Galveston, closer to the geographical center of the United States. All these valiant exertions managed to spirit a few immigrants away from the overpopulated areas, but the four or five thousand subtracted each year made no noticeable difference in the metropolitan accumulations.

These organized drives failed to achieve more removals than they did (between 1901 and 1912 the Industrial Removal Office sent out of New York 59,729 people to 1,474 towns) because they focused on moving the wage earner, who was economically better off near the source of employment in the largest cities. A contemporary pointed out, "the progress made by this movement is controlled almost exclusively by economic conditions. Thus, cyclical fluctuations of labor demand are reflected in the number of removals."

Quite another process did spread some 35 per cent of America's Jews outside New York, Chicago, Philadelphia, and Boston. From the very earliest years of immigration, Jewish settlement involved a kind of mobility that was at once spatial and social. The laboring man found no incentive to leave New York, but one who was about to become a businessman did. A peddler in his travels saw and liked another town, a worker with savings heard from a friend, a grocer not doing so well read in a newspaper—somehow, they learned that an opportunity existed, and were off to test it. So it had been in the seventeenth century, and so it remained in the twentieth.

From these people and their descendants came the bulk of the Jewish population in the rest of America. The fact that they or their antecedents were often independent merchants accounted for the very low proportion of proletarians outside the largest cities and for the very high proportion of proprietors and people in other middle-class occupations. Probably a majority settled in cities with ten thousand Jews or more, places like Cincinnati, Cleveland, Detroit, Los Angeles, Baltimore, St. Louis, and Minneapolis. Although there were not enough Jews in these cities to support the full range of communal activities that flourished in New York, there were enough to maintain synagogues and philanthropies.

Because of the structure of their population, the history of these communities was somewhat different from that of the largest ones. As in New York and Chicago, there was a focal point of primary immigrant settlement, a place where the newcomers initially found homes and where they built their first institutions. Although not as crowded as the East Side, and with fewer features of the slum, these districts had many of the same social characteristics.

The same urge to escape led the more prosperous away here too, but it was a different kind of outward movement. Since the economic status of such people improved more quickly, they sought better homes earlier. The relative sparseness of numbers made it difficult to maintain more than one Jewish area, and those who moved were likely to plant themselves in the midst of other ethnic groups. The consequence was a sharper break, and often the only ties that survived were those which grew out of the desire, or compulsion, to continue to support religious and charitable organizations. In this context communal life was likely to be narrower, if more formal and more tightly organized, than in the largest cities.

Less frequently than earlier did the Jews wander off to the smaller towns of America. The county seat or market town with a population of ten thousand or so had by now passed the peak of its importance. There were fewer opportunities now in such towns to attract the newcomer, and the brighter youngsters were moving off to the larger places. Here and there clusters of Jewish families remained, joined occasionally by additions from the big cities, but more often losing strength through intermarriage or the gradual dissolution of religious or sentimental ties.

The shift of emphasis to the metropolis was the outcome of the change in character of the country and of the immigrants who came to it. The new circumstances set serious problems before Americans who now had to orient all social and communal institutions toward the necessities of urban life. For almost fifty years after 1870 the Jews of the United States, themselves changing, attempted also to keep pace with the swiftly developing trends of American society. Old residents and newcomers tried, each in their own fashion, to make the adaptation, and discovered, in the process, a basis for meaningful cooperation with one another.

CHAPTER SIX

Two Communities: 1870-1919

In the rapidly expanding social order after 1870 there was room enough for every diversity. The appearance of strangers did not at first perturb the Jews already established in a comfortable Americanism. There seemed no reason why several kinds of Jews should not live side by side together. The experience of other groups offered ample precedent. But in the last decades of the nineteenth century a second community emerged, built by the immigrant Jews who could not identify themselves with those long settled in the country.

The older community was by then stabilized. It had a variety of interests, but its members were likely to argue that in time the one link that would hold them together as a group and would divide them from other Americans would be that of religious affiliation.

The temper of the aggressive reform movement was such as to hasten the process of social conformity. In 1870 the reform leaders did not consider themselves a distinct sect within American Judaism. Rather, they thought, they were the vanguard of a trend that all synagogues would in time follow. It was necessary only to further the specific revisions of ritual and practice that would accommodate Judaism to American life.

The reform leaders aspired, above all, to recruit a native rabbinate that would bring order to the chaotic affairs of the autonomous and leaderless congregations and that would approach religious problems without the biases of a European background. Efforts to establish a seminary antedated the Civil War. However, Isaac M. Wise had not then been able to keep Zion College open in Cincinnati more than a few years. Shortly after the war, Maimonides College of Philadelphia survived all of six years, but graduated only one student. In New York, David Einhorn's project never came to life. Then and later the stumbling block was that careers in the rabbinate were not such as to attract the best talent, and theological schools could not survive without the active support of some national organization.

Aware of that necessity, Isaac M. Wise and others had long labored to create such a body. Their efforts finally resulted, in 1873, in creation of the Union of American Hebrew Congregations, a body with which existing congregations of many shades of belief and practice were affiliated. The Union two years later was responsible for opening the Hebrew Union College in Cincinnati, organized for the purpose of educating an American rabbinate.

The hopes for reforming those settled Jews who were still orthodox were frustrated. Although all the synagogues had been adjusting themselves in varying degrees to the American scene, a single organization was not capable of holding together all the varieties of Jews. Irritating incidents kept the orthodox on their guard. At the famous Highland House banquet of 1883, held to celebrate the first Hebrew Union College commencement, an oversight brought shrimp to the tables of the diners and horrified those in attendance who observed the laws of dietary *kashruth*.

The formulation shortly thereafter of an ideology of reform precipitated a clear-cut division of the old Jewish congregations into two distinct groups. The reform rabbis, often German or educated in Germany, were not satisfied with a gradual accommodation; they sought as well the satisfaction of a consistent theological system to account for and to justify the changes in practice. At Pittsburgh in 1885, the Central Conference of American Rabbis, under the leadership of Kaufman Kohler, adopted such a statement of principles, one that stressed the position of the Jews as a religious, not a national, community and rejected, even as an ideal eventuality, the notion of a messianic return to Palestine.

The statement was unacceptable to a substantial group which withdrew under the guidance of Sabato Morais, rabbi of one of the oldest Sephardic orthodox congregations in Philadelphia. A number of factors antagonized the dissidents. As individuals they were dissatisfied with the existing leadership. Local interests in New York and Philadelphia were unhappy that the control of Jewish religious life was vested in Cincinnati. But most galling was the attempt to state in ideological terms the meaning of changes that had imperceptibly grown in practice. Such a statement was frightening because it revealed the extent to which their Judaism, despite professions of orthodoxy, had already been transformed.

Those who broke away from the Central Conference on occasion referred to themselves as orthodox. But their orthodoxy was far from that of their parents and remote also from that of the immigrant Jews from eastern Europe. Consequently, they preferred the designation, "historical" Judaism, or later that of "conservative" Judaism. They proceeded, in the years that followed, to create a parallel set of organizations, with their center at the Jewish Theological Seminary of America, established in 1887 in New York. Abjuring, for a time, all ideology and free of much of the self-questioning of the reform movement, the conservatives nevertheless discovered that their pattern of accommodation differed only in degree from reform patterns. Often the very same men supported both causes, serving, at the same time, as trustees of reform temples and of the Jewish Theological Seminary.

Whether reform or conservative, these Jews continued in other organizations the features already adopted, those now common to all native Americans. The Jews of this generation maintained the impressive array of institutions established earlier, and also added to them. The old lodges and fraternal organizations persisted, becoming increasingly native in composition. At the same time newer organizations emulated the gentlemen's clubs and the women's circles of upper-class society. Literary and cultural associations were more common than before, as were groups devoted to young people. Thus the appearance of numerous patriotic and historical societies in the 1880s and 1890s led to the foundation of the American Jewish Historical Society in 1892. Again, the spread of the YMCA in the last quarter of the century led, by imitation, to the foundation of the YMHA. After World War I, Jewish golf and country clubs would similarly make an appearance.

As a matter of course both reform and conservative groups continued to expand their philanthropic ventures. Works of charity and agencies to assist the dependent were mostly in

America the province of voluntary associations, Jewish as well as Catholic, Lutheran, Baptist, or nondenominational. The care of the ill received more attention than earlier, stimulated by the development of modern medicine and by the increase in the number of Jewish doctors. Mt. Sinai in New York, Michael Reese in Chicago, Mt. Zion in San Francisco, Beth Israel in Boston, Cedars of Lebanon in Los Angeles were among the better-known hospitals. Numerous sanitaria and clinics supplemented their work.

Among the helpless were also the aged and the very young. After 1865 there were homes in Philadelphia and New York for elderly Jews, unable any longer to support themselves, too aged to adjust still further to American ways, and a drain upon the limited resources of relatives. Before the end of the century similar institutions operated in twelve different cities. By the same time, orphanages had been erected in fourteen places. Still other groups set themselves the task of ministering to the wayward and redeeming the errant; societies to aid prisoners, to deal with juvenile delinquency, desertion, and family welfare developed steadily. These philanthropic and social activities created no problems of self-identification. Innumerable groups of other religious or national antecedents likewise performed these functions for themselves.

This array of institutions, impressive as it was, did not satisfy the Jews of eastern Europe. Coming ashore, these newcomers were strangers as other immigrants had been before them—not much less strangers to the Jews already settled than to other Americans. The new arrivals therefore labored under the familiar urgency to create an institutional life of their own.

For many of these religion was, as it had been at home, a central concern. They found none of the existing synagogues adequate, neither the reform nor the conservative nor the American orthodox. They sought instead to recreate that which had been unique to their specific home in the Old World, and since their settlement concentrated them in the largest cities, they found ample opportunity to do so. The result was a phenomenal multiplication of synagogues; in New York, the fourteen of 1854 had become almost one hundred and fifty in 1890, more than three hundred in 1900 and more than twelve hundred in 1942.

The number may have been even larger. Who could count them, tucked away as they were in the unexpected corners of the metropolis? The building itself was only incidental, and limited finances rarely permitted one of these congregations the luxury of erecting a structure for its own use. Sometimes the little society was fortunate and found for sale a church whose former tenants had fled the district as the immigrants occupied it. More often an empty hall was made to serve. And frequently enough the curtained windows of a store front hid the bearded faces of the men stooped at study or swaying to the inner rhythm of the evening prayer.

Nor did these synagogues boast elaborate staffs. The eastern European rabbis were slow to join the migration and only the most prosperous congregations could afford to pay their modest salaries. By 1920 less than half these places of worship were thus ministered to.

Not many more had a cantor regularly in their employ; and a meager salary usually compelled him to eke out his livelihood as a teacher or marriage celebrant or by working at

Judah P. Benjamin (right), United States Senator from Louisiana, 1852–1860, became Attorney General, Secretary of War, and Secretary of State under the Confederacy. . . . Isaac M. Wise, about the year 1860, when this eminent rabbi was the leader of the K. K. Benai Yeshurun in Cincinnati. (Courtesy of American Jewish Archives.)

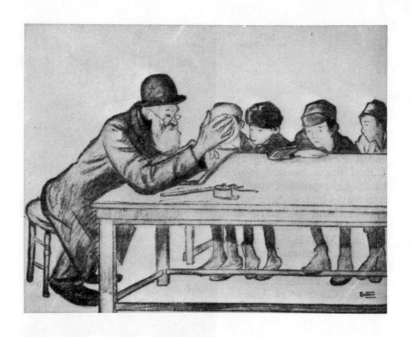

חג האסיף.
(ניו יארקער פארמערס).

A drawing by Jacob Epstein, of the *cheder*, regular religious classes conducted mostly in the Jewish quarters of the large cities after 1880. (From *Spirit of the Ghetto* by Hutchins Hapgood, New York, 1903.) . . . Jewish immigrants, seldom tempted by the life of a farmer, attempted to establish farm colonies in New Jersey and elsewhere at the turn of the century, but their main income came from summer boarders. The cartoon—"Jewish farmers rejoice in a harvest of summer boarders"—is from *The Big Stick*, October 17, 1913.

the sewing machine between the Sabbaths. Yet no congregation was so poor as to forego the services of a *hazan* at the great holidays. There was then much scurrying about and frequent auditions to be sure the limited fee brought the utmost value. But on these occasions the clear tones and piercing trills of the cantor more than repaid his cost. As he let forth the great blasts of climactic supplication, he became indeed the emissary pleading for each man before a familiar God.

Day to day and week to week, however, the *shul*, or synagogue, was managed by its beadle, the *shamas*. A somewhat comic figure who was everyone's servitor, he nevertheless frequently held an exaggerated view of his own importance. Often he lived with his wife and helpmate in quarters attached to the place of worship which he fitfully essayed to keep clean and in shape. It was he who supervised the order of the service and dealt with the needs of the members. He too on occasion was a teacher of unruly youngsters, and he learned to supplement his income by a variety of desperate expedients.

While the synagogues were ill supplied and haphazardly staffed, a substantial number of religious functionaries made a living for themselves without affiliation with any institution. The *shohet*, or ritual slaughterer, if he were fortunate, landed a steady job with the meat packers; if he were not, he stood in the feathery market as the women brought along their squawking Sabbath dinners about to be fresh-killed. The *mohel*, or ritual circumciser, and the *maschgiach*, or inspector of dietary regulations, similarly rendered their services for fees. The operations of these religious free lances were evidence of the degree to which the European Jewish community had been disrupted in America, with each of its functions independently falling to whoever would assume them.

With many rival authorities in competition, the ordinary Jew was not likely to trouble himself with punctilious obedience to any. Only in New York and Philadelphia, for a few years, were there attempts to set up formal community organizations, and the ultimate failure of these *Kehilloth* discouraged others from following. Generally a few congregations, or a committee of rabbis like the one in New York in 1888 under Rabbi Jacob Joseph of Vilna, might unite for such specific purposes as the supervision of ritual slaughter and the examination of *mohelim*. And some, though not all, joined one or another of such national federations as the Jewish Ministers Cantors Association. But any more rigid entanglements were avoided.

The disruption of old forms was critical when it came to education. The religious upbringing of the young was of first importance to the orthodox; yet the old familiar ways of religious education were inadequate in the New World. The traditional forms here became entangled with new objectives and lost their original shape and meaning.

The orthodox eastern Europeans, in whose lives *cheder* and *yeshiva* had played so prominent a part, tried to carry those institutions to the new land. But in America it was difficult to keep young people to the study of Torah, *lishmo*, for its own sake. For parents and children alike, the prospect that education might open a way out of the life of labor in shop or store was both exciting and disturbing. Furthermore, compulsory-education laws, in New York in 1904, and elsewhere later, imposed conditions and specified a secular curriculum that the traditional *cheder*, which devoted full time to the sacred language, could not meet.

All but a few of the immigrants and their children, therefore, relied on the public schools for elementary and secondary education. Only thus could they afford a training which was in any case expensive enough. Not many families could spare even a minimal levy upon their budget for this purpose or, more crucial, the loss of earnings when youngsters were thus made unproductive. Many students, to help themselves, attended night schools or worked after hours to make up the difference.

The problem of financing a college education was still more difficult. Yet by World War I 15,000 Jews were college students and twenty years later more than 100,000, one-tenth the national total. Some took advantage of the free institutions such as the city colleges in New York; others drove themselves hard in the quest for scholarships; and still others managed to get higher education through their own part-time labor. Still, probably the greatest number attended through the sacrifices of their immigrant parents who hoped thus to open the way to their children's rise to professional status. Thus, talk of a Jewish university, mentioned as early as 1854, and bruited about again in 1902 and 1922, came to nothing. The college degree was a purely American accessory, a token of acceptance by the outside world. Bestowed from within the group, it lost its magic.

Jewish educational activities thus became supplementary. These folk took the public-school system as a logical base and built about that. The religious aspects of education of course could not be shifted to other hands. The very separation of church and state compelled every denomination to make its own provisions for training its youth. The Jews, accepting the condition that the major proportion of their children's time would be spent in general studies in the public schools, were driven to devise a means of adding the traditional lore to those studies. Although they had had a long experience with education, this problem was new.

The first recourse was an adaptation of European methods. Earlier, some established Jewish families had hired tutors to instruct their children in the elements of Hebrew and in the basic religious precepts. Now the *melamed*, quite another type of teacher, became a familiar figure. Regularly he knocked at the door, to be admitted by the harried mother who had just cleared the kitchen table for his coming. The assembled boys watched him free the books from the leather thong, and then they were off in singsong rehearsal of the sacred letters, while the baby brother peeked curiously from behind the wash tub.

The more enterprising instructors assembled enough students to conduct religious classes which met after school hours and which they called a *cheder*, after the manner of the old country. Usually independent of the synagogue, meeting in the teacher's own apartment or in a vacant store or basement, they were uniformly unsuccessful. There was little about them that would attract an American youngster while other children were free to use the same time at play. Instruction was in Yiddish; it was backward in methods, and it relied for incentive upon the disciplinary value of the *rebbe's* good right arm wielding the leather strap. And the *rebbe* himself, alas, less often felt the call to teach out of the wealth of his knowledge than out of the poverty of his other means of earning a livelihood.

Although the *cheders* sprouted by the hundreds in the Jewish quarters of the large cities after 1880, they affected relatively few children, and those, often only for the brief period of preparation for the *bar mitzvah*, when, at thirteen, the boy became a man. It was a shock, but hardly a surprise, when Jews learned from a survey by Samson Benderly that in 1908 only 28 per cent of the Jewish children in New York between the ages of six and sixteen received even the scantiest Jewish education.

Yet if the *cheder* did not please the children, its American substitutes did not satisfy the parents. The Sunday and congregational schools that had already developed among native Jews seemed, to the immigrant, no solution at all. Attached to synagogues that appeared at least dubious in their orthodoxy, if not out-and-out reformed, these institutions were judged utterly inadequate by the transplanted European. Thus the immigrant sought to forge independently the links he deemed essential to tie his sons to the old tradition.

The solution, in so far as a solution ever emerged, came with the development of a part-time school, conducted after public-school hours, that used English as the language of instruction, that was modern in pedagogical methods, that was coeducational, but yet was adequate in content. That is, it stressed the study of Hebrew and was sufficiently orthodox. In the Machzike Talmud Torah after 1883, Pesach Rosenblatt had experimented with such a course, as had Harris Horwich in Chicago somewhat later. Through the influence of these examples, but independently, such schools spread through all the large cities, particularly after the turn of the century. In terms of the number of students enrolled, they were at that time still outdistanced by the *cheder*, but the trend of the times was with them; they continued to grow while the older type entered upon a decline. In 1935 the Talmud Torahs of New York boasted 110,000 students, the *cheders* only 12,000. By then, in the larger places, there were also Hebrew high schools, always supplementary to the public high school, which carried such religious education to the secondary level. Teachers for all these schools were being prepared at Gratz College in Philadelphia, and at several other teacher-training institutes.

Development of higher Jewish education was slower in coming since that called for full-time study. Yet the immigrants could not conceive that the American Jewish theological seminaries, developed in the reform and conservative traditions, could take the place of the European *yeshiva* where scholars, supported by the community, devoted themselves exclusively to study for its own sake. Imbued with that older ideal, a group of Jews had organized the Yeshiva Etz Chaim in New York in 1886, but that institution never managed to develop its instruction above a very elementary level. Not for another eleven years did the desire approach fulfillment with the creation of the Isaac Elchanan Yeshiva, also in New York.

Yet the *yeshiva* did not evolve in the form that the immigrants had anticipated. In America, the students were not so easily satisfied to live off the bread of the Torah; they insisted upon a course of study that would lead to a definite goal, the rabbinate. They also wanted the privilege of pursuing more general studies in addition to the talmudic ones. In 1908 serious differences between directors and students became an open conflict. A break was averted, but the *yeshiva* became an institute for training orthodox rabbis and teachers of Hebrew. Despite the distrust of secular subjects, the students were also allowed to register in the public high schools and colleges until the *yeshiva* itself made provision for such supplementary instruction within its own walls.

Just as the Jews of eastern Europe had found existing religious institutions inadequate to their needs, so too they would often not be content with the social and cultural associations they discovered on arrival. Upon landing, they usually set themselves the task of creating new ones.

Some of the newcomers were ready to participate at once in the general cultural activities of the United States. Others involved themselves in associations and clubs that also took in their *landsmen*, whether of the same religious affiliation or not. Thus, Romanian Jews formed the backbone of the Carmen Sylva Association in New York, a nonsectarian society named after the queen of their former homeland and dedicated to the study of its literature. Similarly, Jewish intellectuals played a prominent role in Russian radical circles in the late nineteenth century and in the first two decades of the twentieth century.

But the east European Jews generally did not have in these matters as wide a range of choices as their predecessors earlier in the century. It was much harder for such people to be loyal to their native lands, even in a cultural sense, while the eastern European governments pursued an openly anti-Semitic policy.

Furthermore, the "Russian" Jews were more alone in coming than had been those from Germany, who had found flourishing German cultural institutions already in existence upon their arrival. When non-Jewish Russians, Poles, Hungarians, and Romanians did begin to reach the United States in large numbers, they were peasants, slow to develop the same interests as the Jews already here. In consequence, the cultural organizations that were evolved by Jewish immigrants at the end of the nineteenth century were often more specifically Jewish than those fashioned by their German predecessors fifty years earlier.

Yet the form was generally similar, dictated by the needs of the environment. The desire for membership in benevolent associations and fraternal orders sprang, as earlier, from the exposed position of immigrants in a strange place. The older organizations were remote and hardly receptive. B'nai B'rith, for instance, despite the intention of its founder, Henry Jonas, became predominantly "German," and in Chicago by the end of the century Polish and Russian Jews complained they were blackballed because of their national origins.

Consequently the number of lodges grew by leaps and bounds, as the new arrivals set up competing bodies such as the Free Sons of Israel, the Sons of Benjamin, and many more, often with only a few offshoots, sometimes confined to a single locality. In addition, there were literally hundreds of coteries even narrower in membership, *landsmannschaften*, and regional and family societies, to say nothing of their feminine counterparts, the ladies auxiliaries that arose as housewives began to acquire the leisure to match the activity of their husbands.

In describing these organized societies there is danger of forgetting that there was often more vitality in aggregations that had no constitutions, by-laws, or officers, groups that were held together only by the fact that they played an important part in the lives of their members. From time to time a club is immortalized by a reference in a written source. It printed its by-laws, or published a souvenir program for its ball, or contributed as a group to some fund. But surely many more that never attained that dignity were worthy of it in terms of the comfort and solace they furnished to lonely immigrants. What their specific functions were is indeterminate; what the Roumanisch-Amerikanischer Brüderbund did in New York in the 1880s is not really known, but perhaps its activities are not so important as the mere fact that the association existed.

Nor must the three hundred coffee-and-cake establishments that flourished on New York's lower East Side in 1905 be overlooked. Surely it was the talk and comradeship rather than the food alone that drew men there. In this perspective, it was a momentous occasion when the first Romanian-Jewish restaurant opened its doors on Hester Street in 1884. Within two decades it had a hundred and fifty competitors in New York alone, brothers under the skin to the more modish uptown clubs, Harmony, Phoenix, Standard, to which the elite Jews withdrew. And when it comes to the completely occasional institutions—say, the halls (Manors, Mansions) in which weddings were celebrated—then the hesitant pen of the historian runs completely dry.

Amidst the confused bustle of the city the newcomer sought any aid that might help him to locate himself. His social and cultural associations were a comfort. But he needed also a reliable guide that could assist him in the face of the new and unusual choices he confronted. That guide was the newspaper.

For earlier immigrants, and for native Jews now, the Jewish press had been supplemental only, read in addition to the English or German dailies from which they drew the news of the day. Indeed, quite a few Jews were prominent in the management of such influential dailies—Joseph Pulitzer of the *St. Louis Post-Dispatch* and Joseph Cohn of the New Orleans *Deutsche Courier*, to name only two. Some, like I. A. Hourwitch, played an important part in Russian-American journalism.

The east European immigration at first made no difference in this field. The journals founded by the intellectuals were, among the new immigrants, very much like their earlier counterparts, not complete newspapers. Only the language was different. *Hatzofeh Beeretz Hahadasha* (1870–1876) appeared in Hebrew, the language of the Russian-Jewish enlightenment. On the other hand, the radical papers, like the *Arbeiter Zeitung*, organ of the Socialist Labor Party (1890), came out in Yiddish, the language of the Jewish laboring masses. The Levantine Jews had their own Ladino journals, *La America* and *La Aguila*.

The decisive departure came with the growth of the Jewish population making possible a Yiddish daily press which would supply complete newspaper coverage. In New York, a series of short-lived trials beginning with *Die Post* (1870) led finally to the establishment by K. Z. Sarasohn of the *Tageblatt* (*Jewish Daily News*), a paper which represented a rather orthodox point of view. As immigration grew, the reading habit developed at the same time and there was room for diversity. In the next quarter-century a dozen or so Yiddish dailies made their appearance in New York and elsewhere, not all of which

survived. Intellectuals connected with the labor movement in
1894 set up *Das Abendblatt* (*Evening News*), which, three
years later, became *The Daily Forward,* ultimately the largest
in circulation and, in policy, the organ of the Socialist Party.
Another voice of orthodoxy emerged in 1901 when Jacob
Sapperstein founded the *Jewish Morning Journal.* Intermediate political positions were taken by *Der Wahrheit* (1905)
and the *Day* (1914), while the new Communist Party in the
1920s sponsored the *Freiheit.*

For many years, the towering figure of Yiddish journalism
was Abraham Cahan. Cahan had come over from Russia in
1882, a wild young man of twenty-two, angry with the Old
World of injustices, his mind stuffed with radical new ideas.
He spent a few years drifting at the intellectual edge of the
labor movement and Jewish journalism, then found his opportunity when he was taken on as a reporter for the New York
Commercial Advertiser. In 1897 this was the most stimulating
journal in the city, alive, intelligent, crusading. On its staff
were a corps of bright young men who were to make their
mark including Lincoln Steffens and Hutchins Hapgood. To
them, Cahan gave an insight into the life of the immigrants;
from them he acquired his conception of the American progressive movement and of the social problems of the United
States.

In 1902 Cahan became editor of the *Forward.* Through
that newspaper, his ideas influenced a wide immigrant following. Cahan was in his own special way a socialist, but scarcely
a revolutionary. His pen was bitter when it described the concrete evils of tenement or sweatshop, but saccharine when it
came to the essential verities of family life. At the root of the

disorders of modern society he found the corruptions of the capitalist system. However the cure was not a violent seizure of power but democratic reform—in politics through the Socialist Party and in the factories through labor organization. He thus provided his conservative audience with both an explanation of their troubles and a practical solution for dealing with them. Through a long life that extended to 1951, his vigorous activity made itself felt in Jewish affairs.

Outside New York variety in journalism was rare, although Chicago, at its high point, had three Yiddish dailies, including the *Yiddische Arbeiter Welt* (1908–1920). More generally, such cities as Cleveland, Philadelphia, and Milwaukee found it impossible to support even one daily for any length of time. The business of publishing a newspaper in these particular years grew increasingly expensive, and none could survive without a substantial circulation. Many readers turned to the New York papers, in some one of which they were sure to find their own opinions expressed. An orthodox Chicagoan thus was more likely to prefer old news from the New York *Morning Journal* to fresh news from a local Yiddish socialist paper.

Usually, outside New York, it was the weeklies that succeeded. For a time, many appeared in Yiddish, like Alexander Harkavy's *Der Yiddische Progress* (Baltimore), and *Das Licht* and *Die Yiddische Presse* (Philadelphia). Later, they were more often in English, *The Advocate* and *The Sentinel* (Chicago), *The Jewish Advocate* (Boston), *The Jewish Chronicle* (Detroit), and many others. Sometimes a compromise made room for both languages as in the *California Jewish Voice* (Los Angeles) and the *Jewish Record* (St. Louis).

The widespread development of the weeklies revealed which attractions in the papers really induced the immigrants to part with their precious pennies for this new luxury. Not news for its own sake but the point of view of the newspaper was important. The press was valued because it offered the newcomers a guide to the New World, helped them understand strange issues, interpreted puzzling questions in a trustworthy manner. The press became, above all, an Americanizing agency. The make-up of the Yiddish newspaper reflected the consciousness of that function. News drew the readers' attention only when it was sensationalized and popularized. The emphasis was therefore on "features." There were extensive weekly supplements, and the daily editions also gave over much space to stories, poetry, exhortative articles, advice to the lovelorn, the misunderstood parent, and the homesick. These were impressive indications that Jews in American society could not rely upon the traditional injunction or the ancient household remedy learned in another world. Whether they wished it or not, they could not stand apart from the environment that changed them. As free citizens they were inevitably drawn into a multitude of new activities. Their press was consequential in so far as it furthered their participation.

The form of that participation depended upon both the traditions the newcomers brought with them and the nature of the settlement. Thus Jewish immigrants took less interest in politics than did other immigrants or native Americans. In part that attitude was a heritage from European experience in which the Jew had been divorced from the state; what he saw there of the operations of government did not lead him to believe that much good could come of it. The experience of cross-

ing from the Old World to the New reinforced this precon-
ceived assumption; in passage across many boundaries, the
state appeared, above all, as the creator of artificial, inhuman
barriers.

Everything that happened after his landing strengthened
the distrust with which the Jew approached this matter of politics. The American conceptions of political democracy and
representative government were not familiar to the common
people of any part of Europe. These ideas evoked admiration
and respect once the Jews became acquainted with them, but
at first they did not seem relevant to an immigrant's daily experience. Unfortunately in practice the state was embodied
in the policeman who took the bribe to turn his eyes away
from the store open on Sunday, in the politician who handed
out the peddler's license for a consideration, and in the local
boss at the ballot box, buying votes with a bottle. Better to
keep away from trouble, obey the laws as far as possible, and
have nothing to do with the whole business!

From a practical point of view, there was not much in
politics to attract the Jew. The whisky that was offered for
his vote was not particularly tempting. Nor was he lured by
the patronage; street laborers' jobs did not interest him, and
the higher offices were monopolized by ethnic groups earlier
on the spot. Significantly, there were enough other outlets
open for Jewish talents so that they did not, as did some other
immigrant folk, view politics as the only means for rising in
society.

Consequently Jews tended to avoid the formal machinery
of government. As far as possible they resorted to their own
charities; they preferred informal arbitration to litigation, and

the *Beth Din* of the rabbi to the court of law. In Philadelphia there was for a long time a permanent board of conciliation to settle disputes among Jews.

Sometimes Jews encountered vexing discrepancies between the secular and religious law. With a rabbi's approval, a husband divorced his wife by a simple declaration in writing that he was rid of her. When he remarried, he discovered he was a bigamist in the eyes of the American court which refused to recognize the validity of the *get*, or document, by which he gave himself freedom. To the civil judges who threatened to give these rabbis "the limit," the whole procedure was immoral, for it seemed to "give men the right to marry just as many women as the men want to marry." But to the immigrant who had known no other procedure in Europe, the judges' attitude only proved how arbitrary were the rules of the native lawmakers.

A few Jews in New York and elsewhere held public office, and there were some Tammany clubs that were primarily Jewish in membership. But the most powerful Jewish political figures of the period, Abe Ruef in San Francisco, Czar Bernstein in Cleveland, and Simon Bamberger in Salt Lake City, arose in cities without very large Jewish populations and with the support of other ethnic groups; and there were Jewish governors in Idaho, Oregon, and Utah before there were in New York and Illinois.

The Jewish press tried to stimulate interest in civic affairs. It urged the duty of prompt naturalization and of regular voting. But it could agree on practically nothing else in politics. In New York, the *Tageblatt* and *Morning Journal* were Republican, the *Wahrheit* and the *Day*, Democratic, and the

Forward, after its own fashion, Socialist. The result was a divided Jewish vote and the absence of a Jewish machine, although occasionally a popular figure like Meyer London, through active communal service, built up a following of his own on the East Side of New York. And most Jewish leaders, like Louis Marshall, approved of a state of affairs in which citizens voted more as individuals than as members of the ethnic group. If the Jews of Philadelphia and Boston more often cast their ballots for Republicans than for Democrats, those of New York and Chicago more often voted Democratic than Republican. Mostly, however, in one place or another, the spirit of apathy ruled.

The situation in politics was in marked contrast to that in the labor movement, a sphere in which Jewish working people, through the period of mass immigration, played a consistently prominent part.

Yet if the ultimate measure of success was large, the start was uncertain and slow. The process of economic adjustment in the metropolitan centers had concentrated Jews in a limited number of occupations. Under those conditions ethnic and economic interests could combine to create a powerful *esprit de corps*. But more was involved than that, for similar concentration of other nationalities in other immigrant industries did not have the same result.

Indeed this was a period to discourage unionization. The two decades after 1870 were transitional for the economic system as a whole and therefore confused for labor. While men were continually changing jobs, and the jobs themselves were changing from day to day, there was little possibility of maintaining organizational stability.

Jewish society—uptown view, 1895. A ball at the "Progress Club" in New York, one of the elite Jewish associations of the 1890s. (From *Harpers Weekly*, March 22, 1895.)

The orthodox amenities were preserved even amidst the poverty of the overcrowded lower East Side tenements. This gentleman is preparing for the sabbath in his cellar home. (Courtesy of Jacob A. Riis Collection, Museum of the City of New York.)

Shortly after the end of the Civil War, a national labor union had led a brief existence and then died away, to leave in the field only scattered local craft organizations. After 1879 one such union, the Knights of Labor, enjoyed phenomenal growth. Drawing together a strange agglomeration of idealists, laborers, and reformers, it opened its ranks to all men except lawyers and saloonkeepers, and combined the mumbo jumbo of a lodge with practical agitation for improved working conditions. Its meteoric rise lasted only a decade; thereafter the decline in its membership was precipitate.

The American Federation of Labor took its place, restrictive as to membership, interested only in the skilled crafts, hostile to immigration, and relatively small in numbers until World War I. Meanwhile, on the fringes a host of radicals—anarchists, socialists, and reformers of many hues—offered up to the laborers their own panaceas for the future. A stranger could not readily pick his way safely among all these choices.

Moreover, the Jewish workers were green immigrants, raw from the villages, not sure of what part they should play in these unfamiliar institutions. Watching the ritual of the Knights of Labor, a Jewish immigrant, being initiated, confessed, "Many of us, on seeing the sword, were not sure whether we were all going to be slaughtered or drafted into the army." These men were not likely to be drawn in large numbers to such outlandish organizations unless it was through some known, trustworthy medium.

Large numbers of Jews apparently first made contact with union activity in 1882 when they unwittingly signed on as scabs during the longshoremen's strike in New York. Abe Cahan was authority for the statement that the misled Jews quit as soon as they became aware of what was happening and, horrified, were thereafter consistently labor-conscious.

There were other reasons as well for the development of labor consciousness among them. For one thing, they had the advantage—or usually it proved an advantage—of leadership by a tiny but very aggressive minority of intellectuals and intellectually-minded workers trained in the most advanced trade unions of Europe, men who brought to New York and Chicago experience learned in the Russian *bunds* and in the English labor movement. These thinkers, having escaped from European oppression to the freedom of tenement and sweatshop, were radicals, anarchists, and socialists of many varieties. They regarded the trade union as an instrument in the battle against capitalism, a means of mobilizing the laboring masses for the inevitable struggle for power.

Their job was to get the immigrants into the unions, to disabuse them of the notion that they might escape from the ranks of the workers through peddling or petty trade, to make the idea of organization familiar, and to lower the barrier of language. Toward that end, an intermediate, educational body seemed necessary.

In New York, Chicago, St. Louis, Milwaukee, and elsewhere, the existing unions had already confronted an analogous problem with regard to the German-speaking immigrants. The labor movement in those cities had set up organizations known as the United German Trades to educate the newcomers and to draw them on into the appropriate craft unions. Now it was apparent similar bodies ought to perform the same function for Yiddish-speaking Jews.

In 1885 the Yiddischer Arbeiter Verein made a false start.

Arising in conjunction with various projects to start a radical Yiddish newspaper, this society consisted of capmakers, shop clerks, clothing workers, barbers, and peddlers and, by 1886, had several thousand members in its affiliated sections. But it shot its bolt that year working in the New York mayoralty campaign for the election of Henry George, and collapsed shortly thereafter.

More significant in its consequences was the organization in 1888 of the United Hebrew Trades under the leadership of Magidow, Hillquit, Cahan, and Weinstein. The group at first acted largely as a mutual assistance society. But it also propagandized for unionism, was interested in socialism, and worked for the eight-hour day and the regulation of child labor and the sweatshop. Through it and through similar associations in Chicago, Philadelphia, and Baltimore, Jewish immigrants were led into the primitive unions that were then springing up among the tailors and cloakmakers, the shirtmakers and cap operators, the printers and barbers. Even the leaders of the American Federation of Labor, who disapproved of such an organization based on religious affiliation, perceived that "to organize Hebrew trade unions was the first step in getting those immigrants into the American labor movement."

By 1890 there were already a considerable number of Jews in the craft unions that had taken shape in the preceding ten years. In the Cigarmakers International Union they formed a considerable block along with the Englishmen, Germans, and Bohemians. Some of the garment crafts, particularly the cloakmakers, were well enough organized to run a series of successful strikes between 1888 and 1891.

But in the four years after 1892, the United Hebrew Trades

ran into a crisis that vitally affected its subsequent role in the American labor movement. The intellectual anarchists and socialists, interested in unions not only as the instruments of immediate economic gains but also as the means for enlisting mass support for political ends, then fell under the spell of Daniel De Leon and the Socialist Labor Party. De Leon attempted to use the United Hebrew Trades as a tool for capturing the Knights of Labor. When that failed, he drew the Hebrew Trades into his Socialist Trade and Labor Alliance. Meanwhile the organization was itself torn by struggle between the Socialist-Laborites and a rival group of Social Democrats under Cahan and Hillquit, who wished to affiliate with the American Federation of Labor.

These factional disputes not only confused the membership but subordinated economic to political ends and thereby aroused the distrust of the immigrants. Furthermore some of the intellectuals were atheists and aggressively antireligious, reason enough for the orthodox to shun them. When in 1890 and 1891 a group of radicals openly flaunted their heterodox notions by giving a Yom Kippur Ball, they antagonized the rabbinate and alienated great sectors of potential membership.

The same factors that proved obstacles for the United Hebrew Trades had blocked the rise of any over-all garment union in these years. Through the 1890s a succession of local organizations fought bitter strikes but with no substantial results. Not until 1900 did the factional fires burn themselves out. Then the needle workers fell into line with the dominant trend in the labor movement; under Joseph Barondess they moved into the orbit of the American Federation of Labor.

The Federation by now had come under the decisive dominance of Samuel Gompers. Gompers had come to New York from England, the place of his birth, in 1863, and had moved upward in the ranks of the new unions until he became president of the American Federation of Labor in 1886, a position he held almost without interruption for the rest of his life. Although he had been born a Jew and was an immigrant, he had little contact with the Jewish community and no sympathy for the unskilled immigrants. He himself had gone to work at the age of ten, first as a shoemaker, then to roll cigars. Active in the locals, he finally became an official and then pulled himself up by his own bootstraps to the presidency. He never forgot he owed every advance to craft solidarity. Accepting the permanence of capitalism, he believed unions were bargaining devices, pure and simple, through which labor controlled the supply of skills in order to secure the maximum return for itself. Most of all he distrusted the wild men, the radicals who wished labor to serve some other purpose. No idea was true for Gompers unless it squared with the union card. And it was only when the Jewish laborers had by experience come to his point of view that they joined the main current of organized labor.

The pure and simple unionism of the decades after 1900 lacked the flaming idealism, the genuine humanitarianism, the intellectual sparkle of the earlier period. But it was successful. The International Ladies Garment Workers Union grew steadily in strength until the great strike of 1910 from which emerged the famous protocol with the Cloak, Suit, and Shirt Manufacturers Protective Association. Whatever the difficulties in the actual operation of the machinery of conciliation and arbitration, the agreement embodied a significant conception of collective bargaining. The ILGWU had difficulty for years thereafter but, on the whole, prospered, as did similar organizations in the men's clothing, the hat, and the fur trades. The stability of these basic unions which were to affiliate with the AFL also reinvigorated the United Hebrew Trades. By 1910 eighty-nine unions, with a total of one hundred thousand members, supported the United Hebrew Trades, and the war years boosted the total to fully a quarter-million. Among the incidental products of the movement was an offshoot—radical Jewish nationalism, anti-Zionist, nonreligious, and emphasizing Yiddish in its own schools and cultural institutions.

The success of the Jewish labor movement was measurable not only in terms of degree of organization but in improved living and working conditions. Also contributing to its success was the nature of the industries involved. The Jewish working force was concentrated in light manufacturing, much easier to organize than heavier industry. Their employers were not coal and steel barons, but the proprietors of small cigar-making shops and contractors in the garment trades. The larger clothing factories employed several hundred hands, but the problem of uniting them into a union was not comparable to that in an iron mill or slaughterhouse.

The fact that both owners and employees were Jews also contributed. There was indeed no love lost between the "German" manufacturer and the "Russian" proletarian; common religion, at first, actually heightened friction. But they could at least talk with each other. Capitalists like Joseph Schaffner and Abraham E. Rothstein were not so far removed from those who toiled for them that they could not sympathize with the aspirations of the laborers. Leaders in Jewish affairs, like Louis

Marshall, Louis Brandeis, Rabbi Sabato Morais, and Rabbi David Philipson were ready to intercede in the interests of the good name of the whole community. Such rapport furnished a point of departure for continuing compromise.

But over and above these favorable conditioning elements was the fact that the unions had adjusted to the terms of the American environment. The idealistic and often radical political principles brought from across the Atlantic had given way to pure and simple business unionism. In this whole process of unionization, politics remained peripheral, except in the 1890s when it was disastrous. In the rest of the period, the leaders may have been socialists in their private beliefs, but their ideas did not interfere with the businesslike conduct of union affairs under capitalism.

Like the other associational activities of the Jewish community, the unions were the means through which the immigrants adjusted to the conditions of the new society. Like the synagogues and lodges, they eased the adaptation to life in America. Through these myriad organizations, the newcomer learned comfortably how to get along in the United States without the shock of raw exposure to a completely alien universe.

The east European Jews now acquired the means of expressing their own reactions to the adjustment. An indirect effect of the prosperity of the Yiddish newspapers had been the encouragement they offered to Yiddish literature. In the years just before and just after World War I, many talented writers had drifted to the United States. Stimulated by the newspapers and, in part, supported by contributions to their columns, Sholom Asch, Sholom Aleichem, Abraham Resin,

Peretz Hirschbein, Abraham Cahan, Jonah Rosenfeld, and I. J. Singer made New York a thriving center of Yiddish literary activity. Whatever the sale of their published books, these men maintained a live, warm contact with the sentiments of the immigrant Jews through the immigrant press.

The relationship between the intellectuals' creative activity and the life of the people emerged still more clearly in the case of the theater. In the latter half of the nineteenth century the Yiddish theater became truly popular; it was responsive to the moods, the emotions, and the ideas of its audience, to which it therefore supplied an intimate, meaningful experience.

In those years, the stage was a mass medium, cheap enough so that anyone could afford to attend. Making no demands of literacy or sophistication, its vivid, dramatic presentation provided an easy, quick, and complete release to thousands of tired people who sought there an explanation for the confusion in their minds and the ache in their hearts, or at least, the means of forgetting them.

Some Jews in America had always been attracted to the stage, on both sides of the curtain. The actor's vocation was more open than most; talent was likely to find its level without the impediments that came from low birth or from lack of connections. By the end of the nineteenth century Jews were thoroughly at home in the American and German-American theaters.

As in the case of the press, however, increased numbers made room for a distinctive Jewish form as well. By the end of the nineteenth century, a well-developed Yiddish theater was active in New York and in the other larger cities.

In New York a start was made in the early 1880s. In 1881

there were already some Romanian Jewish actors at the Oriental Theater on the Bowery. A year later, N. M. Shaikevitch and Abraham Goldfadin brought over a troupe from Russia. In 1886 another company of Romanians established themselves at the Roumania Opera House, and within a few years were thriving. At the end of the century there were three Yiddish theaters on the Bowery alone, Jewish Peoples, Thalia, and Windsor, that devoted themselves entirely to the Yiddish drama. With other houses that gave occasional performances, they were estimated to draw at least twenty-five thousand patrons a week.

A comparable development took place outside of New York. In Philadelphia were the Arch Street, the Standard, and the National Theaters; in Chicago, Glickman's and the Yiddische Dramatische Gesellschaft. No slackening of growth was noticeable until after World War I. By then the Yiddish Art Theater had also made its appearance in New York, and there were resident companies in towns as scattered as Chicago, Detroit, Newark, Philadelphia, Cleveland, and Toronto.

In the earliest years, and to some extent throughout the history of the Yiddish theater, its plays were only slightly intellectual. The great attraction was the actor and the whole troupe revolved about the leading star. Jacob P. Adler and Bertha Kalisch, Sigmund Feinman, David Kessler, and Boris Tomashefsky all had their followings and their distinctive roles. The plays were often written for the occasion by dramatists well aware of what the audience wanted to see and hear. Naturally such dramas involved little more than the manipulation of stock plots and situations. If "Professor" Hurwitz managed to turn out almost a play a day over long peri-

ods, that was accomplishment enough; he was not likely to be
criticized for any lack of originality. Even after the reforms
of Jacob Gordin, after serious writers like Kobrin, Libin, and
Singer took up the task, they could not escape the obligation
of dealing with themes on which their audience insisted.

Not that there was necessarily any uniformity in subject
matter. There were plays about the Old World or the New,
historical or contemporary. There were adaptations from
Shakespeare and from the American theater—*The Three
Musketeers, The Black Flag, Two Orphans, Hero, the Indian
Chief.* What was important was that the story should have a
meaning for those who watched it unfold.

And the meanings were those that immigrants found in the
real everyday life about them. The ever-present power of
temptation from material, earthly things that sap faith and
morals, as in Gordin's *God, Man, and the Devil.* The unfaith-
fulness of children who, unmindful of sacrifices in their behalf, turn against their parents. (*King Lear* was a natural for
this theme.) Above all, the sadness of life, the ease with which
hopes were frustrated, the imminence of death that awaited all
men. No device was more effective than a *Kaddish* scene (memorial service for the dead), especially when juxtaposed upon
what, normally, was a happy occasion. The high point of the
"Jewish Hamlet" was described by a program note as the "sad
wedding of *Vigder* (Hamlet) and his dead bride *Esther*
(Ophelia) according to the Jewish religion."

Perhaps it was the inability to supply meanings in terms of
contemporary Jewish life that accounted for the fact that
comedy did not flourish as such and quickly degenerated into
burlesque. What was worse, the Yiddish theater had to com-

pete, as far as comedy was concerned, with vaudeville, then in its period of greatest vogue. The result was the Yiddish musical comedy as set forth by Joseph Lateiner. The true formula for success in this field was ultimately discovered by Sigmund Mogielesco who borrowed ruthlessly from the chants of the Russian cantors, the arias of Italian operas, and the popular song hits of the day, to contrive melanges that still had a Yiddish flavor and were magnetic at the box office. (In the same way, a two-step, though popular dance music, seemed more respectable to the immigrants when its title page gave assurance that it was composed by "H. A. Russotto, author of the original Kol Nidre and other Hebrew melodies.")

The dilution of the Yiddish content of the Yiddish theater, successful at first, was ultimately self-frustrating. It stimulated tastes that could better be satisfied in the more lavish English American theater. As plot and story receded before song and dance, even language became unimportant. But the hardest blow came from without, from the emergence of the movies as a competitor. Although many Jews—Sam Goldwyn, Douglas Fairbanks, Louis B. Mayer, the Warner brothers, and others —participated in the new industry, there was nothing specifically Jewish about their product. Yet that great, inert mass medium, completely neutral in its effects, drew the immigrants away from their own theater. The movies which revealed the golden land, the idealized and romanticized America, had the superior attractiveness of the dream to the reality.

Schools, newspapers, theaters flourished only while they filled some significant need in the life of the Jew in America; the momentum acquired by virtue of having served in the Old World never carried an institution very far. There was no difference, from this point of view, in the Jews who arrived before 1870 and those who arrived after. The size of the numbers involved, the total circumstances of the transition, and the character of the place of settlement introduced variations in the means of expression. But in the last analysis, cultural institutions took form in response to the immigrant's judgment that they served a function in his life in the United States.

It therefore followed as a matter of course that the way of the east European Jew in these years parted company, on so many counts, with that of the "German" Jew, the product of an earlier migration. The necessities of each group had led it, since 1870, to create its own institutional life. The newcomer would no sooner worship on Sunday to the accompaniment of the temple's organ, than the native would be found downtown on his way to the Yiddish theater. They seemed almost to inhabit two distinct communities.

However, in these years also, men out of both communities now and then faced problems that demanded the collaboration of all. Gradually they learned that, although they were not one, they could advantageously work together.

CHAPTER SEVEN

Americanization: 1880–1920

The two communities developed separately; yet they could
not stay apart. For centuries in Hamburg, two groups of Jews
had coexisted without losing their distinctiveness. But the free
and fluid society of the United States did not tolerate the rigid
lines of social division which alone could preserve the distinguishing differences. Subtly, unexpected affiliations created
ever more numerous points of contact; the calls of philanthropy involved them one with another, the pull of Americanization drew them together, and the recognition of common
obligations to overseas Jewry gave them shared interests.
Meanwhile the larger American community, in which native,
German, and east European Jews were alike fixed, thrust before them challenges which they could only meet together.

The older groups of settled Jews had always been aware of
the tragic plight of the eastern Europeans and, swayed by the
same humanitarian impulses as other Americans, had hoped
that the United States might become a place of refuge. Thus in
1869 Rabbi Bernhard Felsenthal, prominent in the reform
movement, in an article in the Russian Hebrew journal, *Ham-
agid*, had urged the persecuted Jews to seek asylum in the
United States.

But the flock that actually descended upon the Americans

in the 1870s and particularly in the 1880s turned out to be not quite what had been expected. The romantic victims of religious persecution, on closer inspection proved to be poor and ignorant, slum dwellers and sweatshop workers, conspicuous in long gabardines and beards, their women disfigured by the Oriental *shaitel* (wig). In the first revulsion, it was hard to tell which was worse, the long-haired anarchist or the side-locked Chasidic rabbi.

This shock no doubt was in part the shock of recognition. The outraged "German" Jew saw, shuffling down the gangplank, himself or his father, stripped of the accessories of respectability. This was what he had escaped from, been Americanized away from; he did not like its catching up with him. In part, the shock came from measuring the newcomers by the standards of the New World, which the native Jews had by then entirely adopted. It was distasteful to incur the ill-feeling of one's fellow citizens on account of these unattractive new Jews; and this unattractiveness, it was frequently pointed out, was "not so much a matter of religion, but of race and of habits." And finally there was a deep suspicion that the backward old Continent, incapable of solving its own problems, would simply dump its expendable Jewish population on America.

In any case, a fear swept over American Jewry lest it be Russified; by 1891 complaints were heard in the convention of the Union of American Hebrew Congregations and of B'nai B'rith that all the gains of the preceding half-century might be wiped out by the newcomers. And before these were even partially absorbed, the Syrians, the Turks, the Moroccans, the black Abyssinian Falashas were on their way.

The shock was less surprising than the recovery from it. For years there had been a failure to conceive the true dimensions of the movement; preparations were being made for fifty when five thousand were already on the way. And there was always the hope that the old and infirm, those incapable of self-support, would remain at home. Yet, like it or not, the American Jews continued to assist the immigrants and continued to fight restrictions upon immigration. The new arrivals were, after all, *glaubensbrüder* (coreligionists) and religion demanded that the way be smoothed for them. A vague, often romantic, impression of the eastern Jew survived the first encounters; he was more scholarly, had preserved tradition in a purer form, and brought to faith a fervor lacking in American worship. All these considerations stiffened the determination of native American Jews to defend these helpless fugitives.

Of this historic obligation of the rich toward the poor Jews such a man as Jacob Schiff was eminently conscious. Raised in the Frankfurt ghetto and later familiar to the banking circles of Europe, he was a maker of railroad and industrial empires. Riches and power were for him not ends in themselves, but means to assist the Jews in performance of a universal mission. He saw himself, the *nogid*, or man of wealth, as a *shtadlan*, or intermediary, between Jews and the rest of the world; and what bound him to Jews everywhere was the conviction "that as Jews we have something precious of high value to mankind in our keeping, that our mission in the world continues, and with it our responsibilities of one for the other." In those words he expressed the sentiments of the successful and powerful men of his generation.

Such thoroughly "German" groups as the Board of Delegates, B'nai B'rith, and the American Jewish Committee therefore continued to insist upon the right of eastern Europeans to come to America, and successive philanthropic ventures labored to raise their status once they landed. In 1909 the last-named organization made a determined effort to exempt the Syrian Jews from the discriminatory laws against Asiatics.

But the gulf between the earlier and later Jews was not easily bridged; misunderstandings lasted a long time. Not that the new Jews were any more coherent or unified a group than those who came in the 1840s. Far from it! There was no love lost between the east Europeans and the Syrians. And what could match the contempt of the Lithuanian for the Galician, the Ukrainian for the Romanian? Yet the similarities in their social experience in America cut all these people off from their predecessors. The economic conflicts between laboring "Russians" and employing "Germans" added to it. And the rich independent institutional and cultural life of the eastern Europeans further separated the two groups. Here and there a prosperous newcomer deserted the ghetto to become a "Daitchuk," but the new immigrants did not easily lower their guard. Their attitude long remained one of suspicion and mistrust.

Yet they too sensed the pull of ambiguous ties. Resentment at the great ones who had deserted the ancient ways mingled with a kind of pride in their achievements; the Schiffs and Guggenheims and Rosenwalds were the symbols of American success and earned a secret respect on that account. For all the jibes, there was nevertheless an expectation that the uptown folk would feel the sense of obligation to aid. Recognition of that relationship supplied a basis on which the old and new communities could draw together. With many a strain in the process, the natives attempted to improve the Russians, by assisting their immigration, by supporting their charities, and by providing facilities for their uplift through education.

Philanthropy established the first direct contacts between the old and the new communities. After 1870 immigrant aid became urgent. As the number of arrivals took on enlarged proportions and as settlement became more difficult, the compulsion to extend organized assistance grew heavier. The process of crossing and resettling was a universal experience; this was a plight every one who had himself suffered it could understand. Furthermore, the fate of the latest immigrants, the "Germans" thought, would reflect upon the general reputation of all Jews among Americans.

The first faltering steps toward easing the way of the wanderers had actually been taken in Europe by the Alliance Israelite Universelle after the cholera epidemic and famine in Russia in 1868 and 1869. But effective measures came only when the pogroms of 1881 showed the urgency of the situation. Then twenty thousand refugees fled to the Austrian border where they accumulated in the town of Brody. Almost at once Jewish societies in England, France, and Germany mobilized their resources to help, and in America, a coordinating Russian Refugee Aid Committee, with branches in New York, Chicago, Philadelphia, and other large cities, set itself the task of receiving the newcomers.

The Russian Jews, once they got here, ceased to be respected objects of sympathy and became pathetic objects of charity. Some Americans never gave up hope that the tide might be dammed up, or at least, diverted elsewhere. Yet the obligation to aid the helpless immigrants was not shirked. The existing Hebrew charity organizations in various places contributed money, and the Baron de Hirsch Fund proved generous in helping immigrants to their destination and in tiding them over until a first job was found. But it became increasingly more apparent that a permanent effort was called for, one that would combine all Jewish resources from both the old and new communities.

In 1884 Jacob Judelson was instrumental in establishing in Philadelphia the Association for the Protection of Jewish Immigrants. Almost at the same time, a Hebrew Sheltering House was set up in New York, and, in the next few years, a series of other organizations joined in the work. A turning point came in 1902 when the Hebrew Immigrant Aid Society (HIAS) appeared and soon thereafter absorbed the sheltering house. HIAS steadily integrated and centralized the administration of aid to the newly arrived. Other groups continued to handle particular aspects of the task; the National Council of Jewish Women, for instance, assumed responsibility for female immigrants. But the core of the Jewish effort was the widespread organization of HIAS.

Coordination of other forms of philanthropy was more difficult to arrive at. Needs grew steadily more pressing with the rise in population and the concentration of Jews in metropolitan areas and in working-class occupations. All budgets climbed astronomically. The United States Hebrew Charities of New York thus more than doubled its expenditures between 1880 and 1895. At the same time the number of institutions devoted to care of the poor and dependent increased seemingly without limit.

The development was neither logical nor coherent. There was often, in these spontaneous organizations, waste, duplication of effort, and inefficiency. Each successive group of immigrants felt the urge to shift for itself once it had accumulated the necessary resources, sometimes sooner. In part the multiplication of agencies was due to the dissatisfaction of the newer arrivals with the lack of orthodoxy of the old, in part to the suspicion that Americans, even Jewish Americans, did not really understand the needs of those who had come from Europe.

Inevitably, the first asylums and hospitals made concessions as far as dietary laws and the observance of the Sabbath were concerned. But the late-comers continued to doubt that they were given a proper voice in the management of the institutions. They complained that their own doctors were not admitted to hospital staffs readily enough, that important offices were never allotted to them, and that their contributions were not adequately appreciated. Since these were not simply agencies for service, but also the means of social activity, each group was irresistibly drawn into more new fields. To complicate matters further, thousands of immigrants continued to bestow their charity in the traditional individual form. In every home were little *pushkes*, collection boxes, through which the pennies flowed to hundreds of causes.

The consequence was that philanthropy, among Jews, could not take on the disciplined hierarchical structure it did among the Catholics. Until the end of the nineteenth century, each agency was strictly on its own; its success depended upon the popularity of its balls and benefits, upon the contacts of its managers, and upon the degree to which it dramatized its appeals.

While no movement got far that attempted to curtail the sovereign individuality of any institution, the glaring weakness of the system when it came to fund raising demanded a remedy. Traditional concepts were not very helpful. Jewish ethics emphasized the virtue of charity as justice, but the obligation was individual and the gift a *mitzvo*, an exercise of personal piety. The worthiest donations were the ones made secretly to unknown beneficiaries, for those were acts of the utmost generosity. These assumptions contributed to the chaos of Jewish philanthropy, for they tended to render the character of the recipient largely irrelevant. Any gift to the most inveterate *schnorrer* was still a *mitzvo* that entered into the reckonings of the world to come.

The premises of contemporary American philanthropy were quite different. Charity to an object unworthy of it was inexcusable, for philanthropy was not a demonstration of piety but an instrument of reform and amelioration. The duty of the generous man was to give systematically so that the recipients of his aid would be able to improve themselves by it. The great Christian philanthropists of the period, Slater, Peabody, and Carnegie held this purpose firmly in view as they created their funds. Similar objectives in time also motivated such Jewish benefactors as Schiff, Rosenwald, and Guggenheim.

The loose conditions of American communal organization had early compelled Jewish congregations and institutions also to apply the test of worthiness. Now the conviction grew that the same criterion ought to be applied to all charity, that the old forms of random donation were dangerous, and that it was necessary to "methodize" Jewish philanthropy.

The solution was to fuse the traditional and the American concepts. The act of giving was still an act of personal piety. But it had to be applied where it would do the most good. In view of the existing institutional chaos, both ends could be best achieved if the gift went to an intermediary that would allocate it by plan to the worthiest cause.

The intermediary agency was a federation which took over the task of raising funds but left the conduct of the affairs of each institution in its own hands. Sometimes two steps were involved, first the separate federation of "German" and "Russian" charities, then union of all. This development appeared first in the cities of moderate size. By 1900 places like Boston, Chicago, Cincinnati, and Detroit had accepted this tolerable compromise between centralization and anarchy. Philadelphia and Baltimore shortly imitated them. But the largest community of all held off for several years longer. The philanthropies of Brooklyn did not federate until 1910. Those in the rest of New York wrangled over their sovereignty seven years more, forfeiting a million-dollar bequest because they could reach no agreement sooner. The amalgamation of the two systems to cover the entire metropolis was delayed for yet another two decades.

Efforts to handle these problems on a national scale had practically no success. A National Conference of Jewish Charities established in 1899 considered such general problems as the handling of transients, family desertion, and tuberculosis in the "dependent classes." But the only substantial achievement in this field was the provision of nationwide support for the Jewish Hospital for Consumptives in Denver. This lack of a national unified effort was not surprising. All these activities were deeply rooted in local conditions and in the local need for activities. The local community was the source of their strength. Any other authority would have been superimposed from without.

The whole process of federation worked counter to tendencies that had kept the two Jewish communities apart. Although the individual institutions retained their autonomy, the broadened base of their support necessarily broadened also the scope of their services. Ultimately the "German" hospitals had to make it possible for the "Russians" to be at ease there. Many a young man or woman condescendingly went down to the docks on the East Side to help the greenhorns, only to find unexpected attachments grow from a comprehension of their difficulties. Leaders of the old and the new groups began to sit on the same boards, discuss the same problems, and opened thus the way to a permanent rapprochement.

With regard to education, the outcome was more complex. Here disparate views of the ends of learning stood in the way of definition of a common attitude. Efforts to come together were seldom successful. Furthermore, education also touched on general problems of Americanization, and those most intimately concerned—the children—were acquiring from the society about them values different from those of either Jewish community. In the long run the cultural development of the children supplied the basis for common interests, but on terms no one envisioned at the start.

The "Germans" and the "Russians" had created two distinct modes of religious training. Having failed to create a separate school system, the former now relied on the Sunday school, the latter on the Talmud Torah. The two systems were worlds apart, with no points of contact.

Secular education, however, offered the opportunity for forging a link. This was one of the means by which the established Jews hoped to assist the new immigrants. To the natives who assumed they knew what was good for the newcomers, the first requisites were those that would prepare the immigrants to become self-supporting respectable citizens. English classes for adults and for children about to enter school were thus commonly provided at once. Next it was essential to supply the unskilled with some mechanical trade. The benevolent thought that far too many Jews lacked usable skills and were dependent upon such uncertain means of support as peddling. Later, it also seemed as if too many of their children unrealistically aspired to places in the professions.

Although the Yiddish press, still influenced by efforts to "productivize" the Jews of the Old World, occasionally supported the emphasis upon mechanical training, the long series of projects to develop technical education for immigrants had few durable results. The Hebrew Free School Association of New York set up an industrial school for girls in 1879 and a Hebrew Technical Institute in 1884, both later a part of the Educational Alliance, and the Baron de Hirsch Fund operated a trade school that prepared students for industrial pursuits. The United Hebrew Charities in New York established a factory where immigrants could learn the garment trade, a project bitterly opposed by workers already in the industry. The Hebrew Education Society of Philadelphia taught cigar making and cloth cutting to men, and millinery and dressmaking to women. Similar organizations flourished in Boston, Chicago, St. Louis, Kansas City, and elsewhere. Since so great a stock was then set upon agriculture, particular pains were taken to develop the farm schools in Doylestown, Pennsylvania and in Woodbine, New Jersey.

These efforts had some direct importance in assisting the newcomers to earn a livelihood, but there was no continuing vitality to them. Adults were too impatient for immediate income to complete a course, despite the fact that they received a small weekly subsistence allowance in some schools. They wandered off to peddling or grasped the first job that came along, whatever their skill, and remained "botched mechanics" the rest of their lives. Quickly the Jewish institutions learned to concentrate on youth. But youth was either just as impatient as their elders or else aspired to higher training. In any case the public schools ultimately took over the function of vocational training, and as soon as the same facilities were available elsewhere, the distinctively Jewish institutions became superfluous.

What other means were at hand for the well-wishers who hoped to improve the newcomers? In this period, occasionally, "Germans" and "Russians" tried to unite to advance the religious education of the immigrant children. The failure to transplant the European schools became more apparent year by year and emphasized the desirability of some action. Dr. Benderly's survey of 1908 induced the New York community to set up the Bureau of Jewish Education in 1910. With similar associations in other cities, many of which ultimately merged into the Jewish Education Association, it labored to create generally acceptable standards, to coordinate activities, and to secure financial assistance.

However native Jews had not achieved for themselves a clear view of the form religious education should take; generally they had simply fallen into the practices of the Protestant Sunday schools. Nor was there a precisely defined conception of the substance these schools would teach. Indeed, in many discussions of curricula, it appeared that the primary objective was simply the general inculcation of ethics and the principles of good behavior.

In time, the whole problem of education became entangled in that of Americanization. Changes in American society began to put unprecedented pressures upon immigrants that ultimately would affect all Jews.

As the nineteenth century drew to a close, some Americans began to question the value of immigration altogether, while others became impatient with the slowness of acculturation. The unconfident discarded the traditional conception of the United States as a melting pot into which many cultures would enter to develop an entirely new one. They insisted that the essential forms of American culture were already fixed, and that it was the task of the immigrant simply to assimilate those forms. They demanded not only "an appreciation of the institutions of this country," but also "absolute forgetfulness of all obligations or connections with other countries because of descent or birth."

That was a demand the Jews and other immigrants of the same period simply could not meet. The choice placed before them was that between the comfort and security of the religious, cultural, and institutional life of their own community and the strange emptiness of an abstract Americanism. The immediate reaction was a stubborn orthodoxy and a clinging to old ways.

The eastern European Jews had not failed to become "Americanized." They had adjusted, they thought, as had all other immigrants, through institutions of their own which provided bridges between the old experience and the new, through being members of lodges, through reading Yiddish newspapers and seeing Yiddish plays. Stubbornness, for them, was simply a hard shell, a protection against the bruises of hostile contacts.

But the consequences of being confronted with that essentially false choice were felt in an acute form by the youth and by the second generation. Boys and girls who went to public schools could not escape the other world around them, and in that other world they were continually being told that the way to acceptance was rejection of the heritage of the past. To a sensitive person like Mary Antin, a young woman whose moving book, *The Promised Land*, described the transition in the 1890s from Poland to Boston, it seemed as if no more was involved in Americanization than the surrender of her Judaism.

For the parents, the danger of losing their treasures, the children, grew greater in these years through the operations of a host of new Americanizing agencies. To the older missions which sought conversion to Christianity were added a number of secular institutions. Religious or secular, all were suspect in the eyes of the orthodox, for all seemed to have the same proselytizing effect.

Among some American social workers in these years the

humanitarian urge to improve the lot of the immigrants took the form of settlement-house work. In the West End House in Boston, the Henry Street Settlement in New York, Hull House and the Maxwell Street Settlement in Chicago, earnest young people came to live among the foreigners, to display, by direct contact, the manner of life of true Americans. With the best intentions in the world, these institutions could not help giving the implication that the old ways were not truly American and were to be discarded.

The native Jews accepted this conception of Americanization and some of them supported the efforts to apply it in the settlement house; regularly Jacob Schiff came to have dinner on Henry Street. In addition, they created other institutions striving toward the same end. Thus the "mission schools" of the National Council of Jewish Women in these years devotedly instructed the children of the poor in the fundamentals of religion—and also in "manners, cleanliness, plain sewing, darning, and patching," as if these were the attributes of Americanization.

The reform rabbis also felt strongly that immigrant children were to be improved through education. Isaac M. Wise had asserted in 1897 that the reform movement represented "the sentiment of American Judaism minus the idiosyncrasies of . . . late immigrants." They conceived of their task as that of ironing out those idiosyncrasies and saw a particularly attractive field for work among the immigrant youth. Promising young Russians, like Joseph Krauskopf and Hyman Enelow, were given scholarships at Hebrew Union College and trained for the rabbinate; there were occasional efforts to open downtown reform synagogues; and, for a time, circuits were set up to take itinerant preachers through districts without reform institutions.

The temple, however, was not equipped for making proselytes. It was remote from the districts in which strangers might wander in. The parents fought it as bitterly as they fought the church. And the young men who drifted away from the faith of their fathers, in these years of growing secularism, were likely to feel no substitute was necessary. In any case, it was easier to drift into a vague lack of affiliation than to take the positive step of joining an institution so much at variance with the practices of their orthodox homes.

The major effort of the natives to influence the immigrant young therefore came through another medium, a Jewish form of settlement-house work. In 1889 a group of Jewish cultural societies organized the Educational Alliance in New York City to Americanize and "humanize" the immigrant Jews. The purpose of the new institution was to eliminate the "Oriental" elements in the life and culture of the eastern Europeans. There was a "People's Synagogue," one which stressed "good citizenship" rather than traditional Judaism. A wide variety of courses were offered in English, domestic science, and civics, as well as, for a while, in various manual trades. In addition, the Educational Alliance sponsored occasional lectures in Yiddish, English, and German; it ran a summer camp and art school, and carried on an extensive program of physical education. Similar organizations arose in Chicago, Philadelphia, and Boston. The YMHAs founded earlier in the nineteenth century as literary and cultural societies, after 1890 turned their attention to service of the children of the immigrants. They came increasingly to collaborate with the Jewish centers that had embarked upon the same kind of projects. On a lesser scale, the Ethical Culture Society also held "downtown meetings," sponsored a People's Institute for work among the newcomers, and established a link with settlement officials by inviting them to a summer school.

Whatever the parents' opinions, these activities were attractive to the children, for they immensely broadened the horizons of the ghetto. But not all those who played at basketball or worked at clay modeling or listened to the lectures, accepted the basic concepts of those who sponsored them. Many in fact still felt a need for solidarity with men of their own kind and were drawn back to the narrower cultural enclaves. By the outbreak of World War I, some such young people had already been influenced by William James's views on group loyalty. They were then receptive to the notions of cultural pluralism and of the federation of nationalities being advocated by James's student, the philosopher Horace Kallen, for those ideas denied the validity of the melting pot analogy and justified the perpetuation of the ethnic group as a permanent feature of American life.

The youths were, of course, not being saved for orthodoxy, and it was that which worried the American orthodox. In the competition for the loyalty of their children, some eastern European Jews—particularly those who had prospered and moved uptown—turned to their own versions of the settlement house to attract the next generation. The hope of reshaping traditional Judaism to appeal to the children of the immigrants after 1900 strongly influenced the conservative movement and the Jewish Theological Seminary. The founders of that movement had hoped to effect a moderate reform in the externals of worship, but one that would not affect the central core of traditional theology. Now they discovered they occupied a strategic position from which to attract the oncoming generation.

There were, in addition, other orthodox religious efforts to hold the American youth: congregational schools, the Jewish Endeavor Societies of New York and Philadelphia, and later, Young Israel. But it was obvious even before World War I, that activities that were solely religious were not adequate to the purpose. To attract the children it was necessary to compete with rival non-Jewish agencies on their own ground.

In 1908 M. M. Kaplan, rabbi of Kehillath Jeshurun, a congregation of well-to-do Russian Jews who were concerned about maintaining the allegiance of their own children, formed the Central Jewish Institute, an experiment in the "modern reconstruction of the synagogue as a social centre." To the place of worship it joined the facilities for a wide variety of social and athletic activities in the hope that the two poles of interest would strengthen each other. In the words of one of its leaders, "While strictly orthodox, it completely surpasses any Reform Temple in modernity of conception." That boast was suggestive; it revealed that the Institute was attempting to accomplish, under other circumstances, what the reform movement had attempted to achieve earlier: the adjustment of Judaism to the contemporary American environment.

This was not an isolated effort. In Chicago, Dr. Yudelson of the South Side Hebrew Congregation was moving in a similar direction; and the years just before and just after World War I saw a notable extension of developments in the center movement, although without strict sectarian affiliations. Imperceptibly, in this form, the influence of the American environment and of earlier reform conceptions played on the new immigrants and gradually established fresh areas of contact between them and the settled Jews.

But none of the new departures stilled the misgivings of the immigrant parents. Of the "uptown" agencies and reform ideas they expected nothing. It was only with reluctance that the Educational Alliance had recognized the existence of Yiddish as a language; and the report of the Hebrew Free School Association in 1894 could, as a matter of course, refer to the *cheder* as "un-American, unrefined, uncultivated, un-everything but Hebraic." Nor were they happy about the conservative dilution of their religion; in this regard Rabbi Philipson noted, with some satisfaction, "that the Orthodox are more embittered against the Conservatives than against the Reformers." But even in his own Jewish center, which remained orthodox, the immigrant still felt a sense of loss and a reluctance to accept change. "The close propinquity of shower bath and religious school seemed sacrilegious to some of the older members of the congregation," a director of one of the centers gravely pointed out.

Basically, all these concepts of Americanization came from outside and had nothing to do with the real life of the immigrant. He could listen until his head reeled to the arguments that proved that Judaism was a religion pure and simple like any other, or alternatively, to those that proved he had two cultures, Jewish and American. All the facts of the living world about him argued to the contrary. His life and culture were one, shaped by experience in the Old World and in the New. To be American meant not to be a greenhorn, to read a newspaper, to go for a picnic, to see a play, to join a lodge —in other words, to do all the things he actually was doing. Whatever others thought, the immigrant never had doubts of his own Americanization. After all, when the Russian considered assimilation for the Eldridge Street Turkish Jews, he thought of the necessity of teaching them Yiddish.

As for his children, his attitude was sadly ambivalent. No doubt he wanted to hold them and shrank from the thought of any weakening of family ties. But he also wanted them to continue further along the way to that elusive Americanization— to find better jobs, live in better quarters, in a better neighborhood; and "better" inevitably meant at least a little bit different. To those raised in the Pale, so much that their children did was foolishness and a waste of time. But perhaps it was necessary, as the *Wahrheit* said in 1913, that their offspring be athletes and frequent clubs so that their characters might "become more polished and refined." If that was so, the Jewish center was preferable to the settlement house.

The children could not fail to be concerned with the business of Americanization. None of the modifications in theory satisfied the basic urge of American Jewish youth for an explanation of its position in American culture. Neither the insistence that Judaism could be like other American churches in practice, nor the assurance that its practice could be compartmentalized into the categories of a dual culture, effaced this second generation's identification of Judaism with the orthodox habits of its immigrant parents. The whole process of its upbringing had emphasized the contrast between "American" and "foreign"; for the children, Judaism was still associated with the foreign.

In practice, therefore, the children did not remain in their parents' communities but, moving outward, sought places in the American society outside the ghetto. Other employments attracted them and other places of residence. They were less likely to retain membership in the old organizations and more likely to seek admission to new ones. The *Daily Forward* and the Yiddish theater did not attract them.

Their own culture, only just emerging, was as yet amorphous. It had recognizable Jewish antecedents, and yet was not often Jewish in subject or tone. Above all, it was expressed in forms familiar to the whole society—the popular press, the vaudeville stage, the theater, and jazz. Adolph S. Ochs and Paul Block, Herbert Bayard Swope and Ernest Gruening, Al Jolson and Florenz Ziegfield, David Belasco and Charles Frohman, Irving Berlin and George Kern, each in his field had moved outside the tight culture of the ancestral group and had established himself without reliance upon specifically Jewish themes or qualities. Although their own heritage demonstrably influenced their work, their contributions transcended all group lines and was comprehensible to men of all backgrounds.

What was true of those who articulated the culture of this period was equally true of those who were its audience, of the readers of the *World*, the spectators at the "Follies," and the whistlers of "Alexander's Ragtime Band." The centripetal pull of common culture was neutralizing the influence of diverse antecedents.

Mass culture did not, however, push Americans into one

homogeneous undifferentiated mass. There were limits within which the realities of American society perpetuated rather than destroyed distinctions. Apart from the sentimental and emotional force of ethnic attachments, some differences in the United States had come to be accepted as permanent and not subject to assimilation—among them those of religion. The young people being drawn away from the "German" Jewish or "Russian" Jewish communities were not often being converted to Christianity. Even when they were altogether indifferent to Judaism, they found it easiest, in the absence of an established church to which to conform, to remain what they were nominally—vaguely Jewish. In so doing, while they left the communities of their parents, they were forming a new community of their own.

The significance of that development was most apparent in the factors that regulated marriage, for this was the critical step that controlled the transmission of the ethnic heritage from generation to generation. The immigrants had opposed intermarriage not simply on religious grounds but also because it disrupted the continuity of the particular group; Lithuanian Jews objected to a German or Galician or Syrian daughter-in-law almost as violently as to a gentile, and to the latter even were she converted. The ability to carry on the familiar line of family life—to speak in the same accents and to cook in the same style—was as important for them as abstract adherence to a faith.

The children, on the other hand, accepted the ideal of *Abie's Irish Rose:* true love triumphant over all. Yet in practice, that acceptance led them more often into marriage with Jews from other neighborhoods, or other classes, or other national backgrounds rather than to marriage with Christians. Increasingly in the United States, marriage for all groups fell into the religious divisions: Catholic, Protestant, and Jewish. The second and third generations, receding from the various Jewish characteristics of their parents, found themselves enclosed in an identification as a single religious group by the realities of the society in which they lived.

One other factor drew the diverse elements of American Jewry together. That was the consciousness of a common concern with the fate of their co-religionists overseas.

The defense of Jewish rights throughout the world had long preoccupied Americans. At various times the Jews, together with many other citizens, had actively protested the infringement of those rights; and time and again the government of the United States officially had acted on behalf of those persecuted or discriminated against. Back in the 1840s there had been vigorous denunciations of the blood libel in Damascus; in the 1850s conversion of an infant against the will of its Jewish parents in the Mortara Case in Italy, and Swiss regulations that discriminated against Jews, had evoked widespread censure; and in 1870 the Senate had spoken out against the reactionary decrees of Romania.

Now too the Jews were vigilant. The Dreyfus Case in France stirred them to action. In 1893 they resisted the extradition of Jewish political prisoners from the United States to Russia. And the long series of pogroms and discriminatory measures in Russia, Romania, Morocco, and Austria elicited their political, moral, and financial support.

Whatever action had been taken in these matters had come at the behest of *ad hoc* groups formed for the purpose of specific protest. Often in the course of agitation, men had felt the absence of some central body capable of speaking for all Jews in such matters. But efforts to form such a body in the nineteenth century on the model of the British Board of Jewish Deputies had foundered on the rock of the real divisions among American Jews.

In the aftermath of the protests to Russia over the horrifying Kishineff massacre of 1905, these problems became more troubling. Many then thought, with Oscar S. Straus, that a plan was necessary "for causing united action . . . in the event of such an emergency" in order to "relieve a few men of great responsibility." At that point, with the memory of recent tragedies fresh, almost everyone agreed that "only one voice should speak in behalf of the Jews in America on matters of national and international importance."

The initiative in forming such an organization was taken in 1906 by Louis Marshall. Marshall was then fifty. Born in Syracuse, he had made one career in the law and was about to enter upon another in public life. His attitude toward Judaism and the Jews was much like that of Schiff and the other men of his generation. He had the time and the inclination to devote himself to public affairs and, unlike Schiff, had also the ability to speak forcefully and to organize complex matters in a precise, thoroughly legal fashion. His attitude toward the eastern Jews was by no means condescending; as an adult he had studied Yiddish the better to understand them. Nor did he have any doubts as to their ultimate Americanization.

Marshall too had acknowledged the utility of a representative body to speak for the Jews; and with that in view took the lead in forming the American Jewish Committee in 1906. But the experience of the next few years taught him that, despite his preconceptions, such an organization was incompatible with the actual situation of the Jews in the United States. The effort to discover a basis for representation revealed irreconcilable divisions that could not be resolved by a simple majority vote. Furthermore, it became clear that such associations by their very nature were voluntary, lacked the means of coercion, and could speak for none but their own members. The American Jewish Committee quickly reconciled itself to the facts.

There were some, however, who still clung to the hope that another, more rigid body might take the Committee's place, or that it would be transformed into such a body. Judah L. Magnes, for instance, was depressed by the anarchy and the disorganization of Jewish life and hoped through some such means to strengthen and revive it. A devoted scholar who had been rabbi of Temple Emanu-El, Dr. Magnes was dismayed by the contrast between American Judaism as it was and his dreams of what it should be; and he was likely to prefer the symmetry of the ideal to the intractable actuality.

Magnes envisaged an American Jewish community strong, united, dedicated to the advancement of culture and to the furtherance of human welfare. He argued that the organization he thought desirable could best grow out of the formation of local governing agencies in the important cities. In 1909, he took the lead in the establishment in New York of such a *Kehillah*.

Dr. Magnes clearly stated the purpose of the *Kehillah*. In an address to the first meeting, he pointed out that, "At the present time there is no representative, authoritative permanent organization that dares speak for the Jewish people," and he complained that consequently "any individual or organization" could "claim to be the spokesman of the Jews." The *Kehillah* in New York, and similar bodies elsewhere, would put an end to the "prevailing anarchy" locally, and form the substructure of a more general national body. The conception proved attractive for other reasons to some orthodox Jews who earlier had attempted to establish an agency with the same name to administer religious regulations.

Quite different impulses moved the small groups of American Zionists in the same direction. The idea that the Jews of the world might, through political action, return immediately to Palestine and establish there a national home had at first not been well received in America. It ran counter to the whole reform movement which rejected the aim of restoration of a Jewish state. The Pittsburgh Conference had eschewed a return to Palestine and had insisted that the Jews did not constitute a nation. The Union of American Hebrew Congregations proclaimed, "America is our Zion," and the Central Conference of American Rabbis in 1896 and 1897 and again in 1912 and 1917 had specifically condemned the Zionist program. The Yiddish labor movement was generally hostile. To the orthodox, moreover, the dispersion had a religious significance: divinely ordained, it was to persist until the Messiah's arrival and was not to be terminated by human, political measures. In a very broad sense, the immigrants had made their choice of a promised land when they came to America. Palestine was not very large in their consciousness.

There was a romantic attachment to the biblical scene that

turned the minds of such people as Mordecai N. Noah, Emma
Lazarus, and Henrietta Szold to Palestine. But significantly
they were not immigrants, rather natives imbued with American ideals. The newcomers were too concerned with their
own problems of settlement to think much of any other homeland. Consequently, although traditional connections were
maintained through messengers and relief funds, the Federation of American Zionists by 1900 had only eight thousand
members in the United States.

Yet there were restless men for whom the movement had
a profound attraction. In 1907 Stephen S. Wise had organized
the Free Synagogue of New York after having rejected a call
to the pulpit of Temple Emanu-El. Although born in Hungary, Wise had spent all but one of his thirty years in the
United States and now burned with a will toward achievement.
Tall and handsome, his piercing eyes set in a striking face, he
preached with resounding power after the style of the Henry
Ward Beechers of his youth. As his resonant voice descended
from the pulpit, it had the capacity to stir the emotions, to
rouse unbounded enthusiasm. His task was to attach that enthusiasm to a cause.

In the Free Synagogue Wise pushed reform to an extreme,
eliminating all but the remnants of Jewish tradition. For
Judaism was to him entirely prophetic and the Jews a people
divinely dedicated to social justice. His own role he conceived
as that of successor to Amos. Consequently he felt an instinc-
tive commitment to liberalism and, without defining his liberalism, embraced in his active career an indiscriminate succession
of causes: labor legislation, single tax, municipal reform, transit
unification, pacifism, recognition of the Soviet Union, the re-

peal of prohibition, and the support of the League of Nations. Indeed, almost every question, in his mind, lost its concreteness and was abstracted in terms of general principles; right conceptions of democracy, freedom, and justice, he believed, could supply the clear answer to all problems.

Zionism, for Wise, embodied all his causes. It afforded the prophetic people its messianic opportunity. In their restored home, Jews could put into practice the just society which would become a model to all nations. To the furtherance of this experiment, he increasingly devoted his energies, though for a full decade without demonstrable results. He too came to believe that greater order and more democratic control in American communal life were necessary to support the Zionist cause. Impatient with the slowness of the masses in following him, Wise came to imagine that a selfish oligarchy somehow stood in the way of attainment of his ideals. Once the power of that oligarchy was destroyed, the American Jews would see the obvious correctness of the Zionist program.

World War I offered the opportunity to bring that desire to fulfillment. For three years all the European great powers were engaged in battle. The Jews of the belligerent countries were immobilized and those of the United States, still neutral, inherited the responsibility for the welfare of the people of their faith everywhere. With the declaration of war against Germany it appeared that America would wield perhaps conclusive influence in determining the outcome of the struggle and the nature of the peace.

Jews certainly had a stake in both. Ferocious battles across the face of eastern Europe had confronted many in Poland

and Russia with immediate problems of relief and rehabilitation. And the treaties, which were to bring democracy and rights of self-determination to areas of the world that had theretofore known little of either, would certainly have to take account of the needs of the Jews. This was altogether apart from the hope of some that the final settlement would make room for Zionist aspirations in Palestine. It could be argued persuasively that the crisis of the war demanded some single, unified, authoritative body to speak for the Jews in dealings with the American and European governments that would determine the future political organization of a good part of the world.

The call of Dr. Magnes and of the New York *Kehillah*, in 1915, for the convocation of a congress of the American Jews therefore fell upon receptive ears. Because of the pressing needs of world Jewry, various groups, attracted for various reasons by the conception of a united community, found irresistible the demand for concord and for direct effort.

The American Jewish Committee approached the idea of a congress with a good deal of hesitation. It was willing to cooperate in any feasible manner, but it hedged its participation in such a conclave with two important reservations. First, it insisted that a congress, if it met, ought to devote itself to specific problems determined in advance. That is, the congress was not to be a representative assembly with general legislative powers, but rather a body limited to specific functions within the areas in which all the participants were in substantial agreement.

Furthermore, the Committee wished the congress to be a

temporary and not a permanent entity. Called into being by an immediate crisis, it was to dissolve as soon as the crisis was over and the need for its functions ceased to exist. The Committee stood firmly, it made clear, on the principle that there was no place in America for anything like "a state within a state."

Although an acrimonious debate revealed the force of the divisions among American Jews, the different groups that entered the American Jewish Congress formed in 1917 accepted these limiting terms. The Congress helped to influence the formulation of the treaties dealing with eastern Europe and with the situation of the Jews in the postwar world. Once the treaties were negotiated its work was ended, and the Congress officially dissolved in 1920.

Substantial achievements were the product of this limited collaboration of the war years. Through the work of the American representatives at the peace conference, provisions were inserted in the treaties guaranteeing the rights of Jews and other minorities in Germany, Poland, and the other signatory territories. Ultimately the League of Nations incorporated into the Palestine mandate the declaration by Lord Balfour on behalf of his Government that the British viewed with favor the creation of a national homeland for the Jews in Palestine. In addition, through other cooperative associations, like the Joint Distribution Committee, the Jews of eastern Europe received the material aid that helped rescue them from postwar desolation.

Yet the collaboration had been limited only, and had not effaced the divisions among American Jews. Like the development of philanthropy and the impress of American culture, the consciousness of the needs of Jews overseas only slowly created areas of common interest and common awareness among the Jews of the United States. Meanwhile, a growing domestic threat to the security of all of them presented a formidable challenge to their capacity to act vigorously yet freely in defense of their rights in America.

CHAPTER EIGHT

Anti-Semitism: 1890–1941

The steady amelioration of the civic and political condition of the Jews in the United States had continued after 1870. The thoroughgoing recognition of equality in law left open only marginal issues. Most frequently the questions raised involved the extent to which old practices in public institutions discriminated against the Jews: Saturday sessions and the reading of the King James Bible in the schools or the position of the chaplaincy in government were examples.

As the century drew to a close, a well-defined conception of the Jew had taken form in the United States, a conception in which he was regarded as a distinctive, recognizable figure, yet one who had an established place in American society. Three elements had contributed to that view: the sense of mystery that traditionally surrounded the Jew, his character as an immigrant, and his identification with the city, trade, and finance.

The elements of the conviction in the United States that there was a strangeness to the Jew were quite different from those of the demoniac character that persisted into nineteenth-century Europe from its medieval past. The emphasis in this country was upon friendly or at least objective interpretations of the mission of Israel which went back at least two hundred years to the reflections of Cotton Mather on the subject.

The visible evidence of mystery was the persistence of Jewry itself. Wonderful in their past achievements, the Jews were "still more wonderful in their preservation." Scattered among the nations, they held to their identity. Like the gulf stream in the ocean of mankind, endless movement did not alter their essential quality. Found throughout the world, they were everywhere alien. Early in the nineteenth century, when news had spread of their presence in Cincinnati, men had come from miles away "for the special purpose of viewing and conversing with some of 'the children of Israel, the holy people of God.'"

The strangeness discernible in Jewish ritual and belief seemed to extend to many unknown realms. The rabbi initiate in the lore of the cabala might possess the power of divination. By the same token, the detective with a Jewish name might uncover a murderer with the aid of "second sight." All sorts of practices had hidden significance. "The Jewish people don't believe in taking life," testified a social worker, "so to all sorts of vermin they use a whisk brush and out it goes out of the window." The functionings of their institutions were likewise obscure. *The Century Magazine,* in a friendly article, asserted that Jews ought to be treated as equals. Yet it incidentally exposed the practices of the *"Kahal"* through which Jews "have always succeeded in driving alien elements from the town . . . where they have settled to get into their hands the capital and immovable property of those places."

There was a purpose to the survival of the group and to the persistence of these differences. In one sense, the Jew retained his identity to serve as the eternal witness of the truth of Christianity. To one Christian advocate of the Jewish return to Palestine, these people were "Jehovah's ever present answer to the innuendoes against the absolute credibility of the Inspiration of the Old Testament."

But there was a larger purpose still, one involved in the Christian concept of salvation. It was a part of the whole scheme of things that the mass conversion of the Jews would herald the second coming. While practical efforts to induce Jews in the United States to change their religion seem to have fallen off after the Civil War, their Christian fellow citizens were still eager to read about such conversions and looked forward with anticipation to ultimate total success. The Rev. Joseph Ingraham dedicated three of his immensely popular novels written in the middle of the century to "the daughters of Israel," to the "Men of Israel," and to "all American Hebrews," in the hope they would see the light.

In a more rational sense, the mission of the Jews was sometimes described as the task of disseminating among all mankind their own peculiar cosmopolitan spirituality and sense of ethics. But that still left a distinctive purpose to their strangeness. If Americans then avidly continued to read Sue's *Wandering Jew*, it was in part at least due to the hold on their minds of its very title and the mysterious image it conjured up.

The vogue of popular novels with a biblical setting added to the atmosphere of mystery that surrounded Jews. Lew Wallace's *Ben Hur* was only the best known of an enormous number of books, the scenes of which were set in ancient Palestine or Babylonia, books which took their readers back in everyday language through the incidents of the Bible. In these stories, Jewish characters appeared in a variety of forms, generally sympathetically portrayed, but in any case, in close connection with the most sacred and mysterious events.

The attributes of mystery were naturally transferred to the present, since Jews had retained their identity from the most ancient times and since their strangeness gave continuing evidence of inexplicable characteristics. This mysterious strain explains the beautiful Jewess who appears so often in the novels of the late nineteenth and early twentieth centuries. She has antecedents, of course, in Shakespeare's Jessica, but she is no mere copy. The American heroine is exquisitely beautiful and distinguished by great nobility of character. Some taint, curse, or fateful misfortune involves her in intricate difficulties which, nevertheless, lead to a happy ending. Often she is juxtaposed with a mean and miserly father, who is, in a sense, her taint, the source through his paternity of her troubles. The mysterious element here is hereditary, in a way, racial.

Descriptions of these mysterious racial ties also took other forms. In 1872 Lynn Linton, a popular English writer of romantic stories, described in a novel the life of a revolutionary who attempted in modern times to pattern his acts upon those of Jesus. To heighten the analogy, the author gave her hero the English version of the name Jesus, Joshua Davidson. The novel was well known in the United States.

Twenty years later, Jesse Jones, a radical New England minister who had his own doctrines of social reform to expound, labored on a novel of the same name, *Joshua Davidson*, that used the same device. However, Jones felt the compulsion to secure for his protagonist a Jewish ancestor, one of "Israel's sacred race," a grandfather, from whom Joshua could learn "as a 'son of the Law,' the sacred Lore of Israel." The injection of this element was significant for it suggested that there was a mysterious body of knowledge available only to "one of the blood."

To the outlines of the picture of the Jew drawn from his mysterious strangeness, were added impressions based on real contacts. As their number in the United States grew throughout the nineteenth century, the Jews became familiar figures in every part of the country. From dealings with them the Christians developed a distinct stereotype, the features of which were determined by the particular condition of the Jews as immigrants.

Like other immigrants, the Jew was a character easily recognized in American society. He could be distinguished from the mass of his fellow citizens physically, both in terms of how he looked and how he spoke. In the mid-nineteenth century there was still a good deal of vagueness about his particular features, however. What seemed then to mark off the Jew most prominently was language and accent. Yet to untutored American ears his manner of speaking was quite like that of other Germans; often he was considered simply a kind of German.

The writings of the New England humorist Charles Follen Adams, in the 1870s, gave most characteristic expression to this early image. The central personage of these popular poems bore the unmistakable name Yawcob Strauss, and spoke an outlandish dialect in which the humor seemed to lie. But Yawcob was not recognizably different from any other German. A shopkeeper, he was pictured in a wholly kindly light, sentimental and goodhearted, preoccupied with his beer and his pipe. The same lack of differentiation was evident in such minor characters as Shonny Schwartz "mit his hair so soft und yellow und his face so blump und mellow."

By the 1890s, however, the stereotype was much more clearly delineated. In the comic magazines of the decade it appeared fully drawn in all its lights and shadows. Occupationally, the Jew was more distinctive than ever. He had by then been identified as a peddler, as an old-clothes dealer, and as a pawnbroker; indeed, the three-ball sign and the title "uncle" were synonymous with him. Distinctive names also set him off: Isaacs or Cohen, Ikey, Jake, or Abie. His appearance was familiar too, pack on back, or holding a basket, or pushing a cart. His garments were either old and shiny with an inevitable black derby hat, or else they were ludicrously new and flashy. His hooked nose stood prominently forth from his bearded face and his accent was thick. Finally, he was invariably concerned with money; the words put into his mouth dealt always with finance and reflected a stingy, grasping temperament. Some Jews were just on the edge of dishonesty like the Bowery shysters, Katch & Pinch. But even a likable chap like Old Isaacs of the Bowery, in the popular play, tells his daughter, "Vhy, I vould trust you mit my life, Rachel. But vid mein money, ach, dot vas different."

There are undoubtedly antecedents of this figure in the older Shylock image, but its specific form came from the contemporary American scene. A dispute over closing hours could bring the charge from a labor leader that the "hoggish Jews" were always after "their pound of flesh."

Whatever its source, by the end of the century this stereotype had been established. Repeated in popular novels, in the press, on the dramatic and vaudeville stage, it made Americans acquainted with a distinctive pattern of physical features, clothing, forms of expression, and language associated with the Jews. Most important, it ascribed to that figure a pervasive concern with money.

These caricatures in the perspective of their later uses have the appearance of anti-Semitic insults, but there is evidence that they were not meant and not taken as such at the time. Innocent of malice, William Dean Howells planned to make one of the unpleasant characters in *The Rise of Silas Lapham* a Jew, but changed his mind when the implications were called to his attention. A public-school teacher in New York could affectionately give *Oliver Twist* to a little Jewish boy as a reward. And as late as 1913, Maurice Levy would unreflectively be described in terms of the prevailing stereotype in Booth Tarkington's popular Penrod stories without derogatory intent.

Here was the critical departure from the Shylock image: the American stereotype involved no hostility, no negative judgment. In a popular story, repeatedly printed in the nineteenth century, Moloch, a moneylender thirsty for revenge, plots to compel a duke's son to marry his niece. The duke's response is not anger, but compassion. In the denouement, he declaims: "Take her, my son, and wear her close to thy heart, for she is a jewel worthy of thy high position. . . . Moloch, where is now thy revenge!" "Thou hast conquered it, my noble Duke," answered Moloch, overcome with surprise and admiration. And everyone lived happily ever after. Indeed, a Jew detective with "the stamp of his race, indelibly traced on the features of all his blood," could, in another romance, win the beautiful Anglo-Saxon heroine, who in assenting declares, "to you I now turn for happiness in life, for your people shall be my people, your creed my creed, and your God my God."

The stereotype of the Jew was, in the 1890s, only one among many. The notion that physical appearance was a sign of national identity was so widely held that a dime novel could speak, as a matter of course, of the New York detective who disguised himself as an Englishman. In the comic magazines the Jew was joined by the drunken, shiftless Irishman, by the sinister Catholic priest, by the gaudy or ragged Negro, by the stupid, soggy German, and by the avaricious Yankees, Mandy and Aminadab. Identified in outward aspects and in dialect as decisively as the Jew, these were intended to be as funny, but no more hostile, than the Mr. Dooley of the same period. Significantly, the Jews themselves accepted the caricature: *Der Yiddischer Puck*, a comic magazine edited and published by the well-known journalist N. M. Schaikevitch, often sketched the identical picture of the Jew as the comic magazines in the English language. In neither case did the picture reflect a deprecatory attitude.

In the 1890s, an additional element took its place in the American picture of the Jew. The impression that Jews were interested in money deepened into the conviction that they controlled the great fortunes of the world. Although the Jews were still sometimes miserly Shylocks, more often they were princes wielding enormous power through their gold.

The newer image was a shadow cast by the prominence of certain Jewish banking houses in Europe. Every American had heard of the Rothschilds and of Lazard Frères. If they had not, an English translation of Edouard Drumont's *La France juive,* published in the United States, gave them long lists of names. Articles in popular magazines devoted considerable space to Jewish millionaires. The exotic figure of Disraeli, "the Empire-making Jew," seemed large in significance, and such intelligent travelers in England as James Russell Lowell were quite ready from what they saw to believe Jews were coming to control the whole world.

By a variety of means, the notion of limitless Jewish wealth gained wide currency. Already in Henry Adams's anonymous novel of 1880 there appeared the opulent Hartbeest Schneidekoupon, "descended from all the kings of Israel and ... prouder than Solomon in his glory." In dime novels the fabulously rich Jew was a stock character. In the midst of depression in 1894 this notion of Jewish wealth was so commonplace that a magazine seriously suggested that the unemployed in the United States would be relieved if only "the trustees of the magnificent fund that Baron Hirsch entrusted to a band of Wall Street bankers" would "loosen the cords about ... [their] money bags."

The wealth of the Jews was ascribed to the fact that they were "a parasitical race, who, producing nothing, fasten on the produce of land and labor and live on it, choking the breath of life out of commerce and industry as sure as the creeper throttles the tree that upholds it." Like the American Jew in a serialized novel, who stayed at his telephone speculating while the world was threatened with destruction, these people were credited with the capacity for profiting from every contingency.

The lines of socialist thinking that connected capitalism

with the Jews, despite the number of them in radical movements, strengthened these conceptions. Thus Laurence Gron-
lund, the foremost exponent in this country of revisionist socialism pointed out in a widely read volume: "Our era may be
called the *Jewish age*. The Jews . . . long ago . . . infused in our
race the idea of one God, and now they have made our whole
race worship a new true God: the Golden Calf. . . . 'Jewism,'
to our mind, best expresses that special curse of our age, *Speculation*."

Still, such judgments were not intrinsically hostile. A tract
that warned "you should not be prejudiced against any race,"
went on to point out that the Jews were naturally money-
changers through no fault of their own, but simply "on account of their excessive shrewdness." Laudatory accounts also
praised the Jews' ability to make money. One of the books to
defend the group boasted: "In finance the Jew has for four
hundred years been the factor that supplied the nations of the
earth with money. The financial system of the world, its in-
vention and perfection, we owe to the Rothschilds." A little
later, a compilation published by the American Hebrew Publishing Company casually remarked: "Of all the nations,
which the world has known, the commercial instinct is strongest and most fully developed in the Jew. He never sacrifices
future opportunity for present gain." If an occasional com-
mentator did point out that the great American bankers were
Christians, that only seemed to stress the internationalism of
the Jews.

As yet these notions were not incompatible with the total
acceptance of Jews as Americans. There were, in these years,
occasional outright slurs against the group, as in General

Grant's Order Number 11 which expelled Jews from behind the Union lines. There were instances of exclusion as when Saratoga's fashionable Grand Union Hotel refused Joseph Seligman accommodations. Sometimes Jews were denied fire insurance on the same terms as gentiles. And a handful of obscure pamphlets were explicitly hostile. But the shocked public repudiation of the slurs and the exclusion indicated how exceptional such instances were. In 1899 Tom Watson, later to achieve racist notoriety in the Frank lynching case, was still vigorously condemning medieval prejudices against the Jews.

In the 1890s an ominous change began. The suspicion took root that Jews were enmeshed in a great international conspiracy, and mounting racial prejudice tinged that obsession with fear and hatred. After two more decades, the finished product appeared—discrimination and open political prejudice.

The roots of the fantasy of a Jewish conspiracy lay in the problems of finance. The growing preoccupation of many Americans with the money question fixed the tie between Jews and finance. In a period of falling prices, disaster was close at hand for great numbers of farmers who, despite mounting production, saw their situation deteriorate steadily, particularly after the depression of 1893. The temptation was well-nigh irresistible to seek a solution in terms of monetary reform. There were still some calls for greenbacks, but increasingly those who agitated for a change in the currency thought of silver. They demanded bimetallism, the free coinage of silver in some established relationship with gold.

In the 1890s these wishes met with an uninterrupted succession of defeats. The rate of silver coinage was not expanded but contracted. President Cleveland's arrangement with J. P. Morgan strengthened the hold of gold, and the election of 1896 confirmed the trend. To make matters worse, silver in that decade was abandoned by almost every other country that still used it—Tunis in 1891, Austria-Hungary in 1892, China in 1896, Japan and Russia in 1897.

Such frustrated reformers as Tom Watson, governor of Georgia, felt the world was plunging hellward, and began to hold the Jew responsible. The defeated Populists acquired a sense of religious intensity about their cause; their speeches became profuse with Christian images. Unable to see any flaw in the rationality of their arguments, they could explain their failures only by the intervention of some external power. The blame was not in themselves, nor in the people in whom they had faith; it must be outside, in England, among the international bankers or—with growing frequency—among the Jews.

The prominence of Montefiore Levi and Alfred de Rothschild in the Brussels Monetary Conference gave the silver men one ground for their suspicion; the activity of Perry Belmont among the gold Democrats gave them another. But they hardly needed evidence. By 1894 the famous *Coin's Financial School* included a map entitled, "The English Octopus. It Feeds on Nothing but Gold." Where England belonged was the simple inscription, Rothschild. In a novel, William Harvey traced the monetary difficulties of the whole world to a plot by "Baron Rothe" to demonetize silver for the sake of English world mastery. A silver tract in 1895 noted as a fact that the Rothschilds owned "one-half the gold in the world, available for use as money, and their aids and satellites own nearly all the remainder."

These spurious theories must have been in the minds of the delirious audience at the Democratic convention the very next year when Bryan ascended to his blood-stirring peroration, "You shall not crucify mankind upon a cross of gold!" The statements advanced by the silver men in the next few years to account for their debacle reveals the extent to which they took refuge in the explanation of a Jewish conspiracy.

They had been beaten, they explained, by the power of an "invisible empire," an "oligarchy" centered in the "mysterious money power" which had bound "the hands of the United States" and had then "proceeded . . . with marvellous rapidity to enslave the human race." Although there was a vagueness in identifying the members of the oligarchy, the Rothschilds were often mentioned and occasionally Shylock openly revealed himself. Thus, one of the reformers, J. C. Ridpath, had Shylock confess his fear of the radicals, and had him point out that the "insurgents will presently turn upon me and my tribe and destroy our business. I must keep my influence with these contemptible Christian nations, else they will cease to support me and my enterprises. My business is to live by the labor of others." The use of such terms was perhaps figurative to begin with, but they certainly received a more literal reading as time went on.

Caesar's Column, a utopian novel by the Populist Ignatius Donnelly, in 1891 had vividly expressed the fears of the future domination of Europe by "the Israelites." Set at a future date, "survival of the fittest" had by then made the aristocracy of the world "almost altogether of Hebrew origin." Christians had earlier subjected the Jews "to the most terrible ordeal of persecution. . . . Only the strong of body, the cunning of brain

. . . the men with capacity to live where a dog would starve, survived the awful trial." The Christian world was thus paying for the sufferings inflicted by their bigoted ancestors "upon a noble race." The great money-getters of the world "rose from dealers in old clothes and peddlers of hats to merchants, to bankers, to princes." They became "as merciless to the Christian as the Christian had been to them." Under the leadership of Prince Cabano, born Jacob Isaacs, the Jewish oligarchy was pushing the world toward destruction.

This oligarchy of Donnelly's fertile imagination bred insurrection, but the brains of the revolutionary organization was also a Jew, a Russian cripple "driven out of his synagogue . . . years ago, for some crimes he had committed." Yet after the uprising, he fled to Judaea, taking with him one hundred million dollars of public funds, with this vast wealth intending to "re-establish the glories of Solomon, and revive the ancient splendors of the Jewish race, in the midst of the ruins of the world."

In this anticipation of things to come was a tone of hysterical fear. The radical urging change yet dreading the effects of change. For Donnelly was no facile optimist as to the possibility of reform. His revolution degenerated into an orgy of destruction which consumed all civilization.

There were specific reasons for the distrust of revolutionary violence. The labor rioting at Homestead, at Coeur d'Alene, and at Pullman in the 1880s and 1890s, and the activities of the anarchists at home and in Europe, had the substantial citizens eager to build armories in the middle of the cities and had even the radicals worried about the dangers of unrestrained socialism.

But more general apprehensions were also involved in the uneasy dread of the future. The implication in *Caesar's Column* was that hidden organizations, conservative *and* radical, worked toward hidden Jewish ends. To that suspicion were later added hazy recollections of similar European charges and confused impressions of what the Zionist Basle Congress of 1897 was up to. The whole contributed to a sense of fear from which the idea of Jewish conspiracy grew, a sense that was repeatedly expressed in other connections as well. The apocalyptic visions of the radicals in these years were often stated in terms of imminence of doom. They envisaged great eras of ruin and destruction that would precede the final redemption and reconstruction of society. Memories of the commune of 1870, scientific descriptions of lost worlds or of the end of this one, the analogy with the reign of anti-Christ that was to precede the second coming, and the figure of Christ himself, all these fed the conviction that suffering was inevitable.

These uneasy conceptions of the future were judgments of the unhappy nature of the present. Certainly in the 1890s there was much that seemed to be changing—and for the worse. For the class in which Edith Wharton grew up, the changes appeared to be a deterioration of culture, and the reaction of that class was fastidiousness in speech and manners. But for the mass of Americans, change took another form.

Through the period change centered in the city, a place of dread and fascination. To the city, and particularly to New York, whole regions of the South and West felt themselves in economic bondage. Yet to the people of those regions, the metropolis was strange; often their only source of information was the lurid detective story. Lacking direct contacts the farmers formed their image of the city not from firsthand knowledge but from gloomy suspicions of its impact upon them.

The cities were unnatural. They worshiped Mammon, not God. They could all burn down, Bryan declaimed, and the great heart of America would still beat. "Embodied paganism," the city was "composed of the people of this world . . . seeking the ends of this world, . . . satiating the animal man with the riches, with the lavish luxury of things." The city, "Babylon the great, the mother of the harlots and of the abominations of the earth . . . drunken with the blood of the saints, and with the blood of the martyrs of Jesus," reigned over the kings of the earth and fed off peoples and multitudes and nations.

This literal fear of the city was characteristic of an era that considered itself rationalistic and scientific and yet took refuge from many problems in the most extravagant faiths. The intellectual reformers, like other Americans, became fascinated by the occult, by spiritualism, mesmerism, theosophy, astrology, and mental healing. To such men it seemed altogether plausible that some alien agency should be responsible for all their tribulations. Not a few writers blamed the Pope or secret societies, and one ingenious author demonstrated that the Jesuits had infiltrated the Masonic societies in order to spread atheism in the United States. In the context of such confused beliefs, the city was indeed a likely butt for the hatred and resentments of disappointed people.

In the United States, the Jews were particularly connected with the city through commerce which was its lifeblood. Coming back in 1907, Henry James was impressed by the alien quality of American cities. He noted "the extent of the Hebrew conquest of New York," a new Jerusalem, and felt sure that the future culture of this country might be beautiful in its own right, but would inevitably be totally strange.

This was the opinion of a widely traveled man of the world. But what did the farmers in the Populist areas think while the mounting burden of debt loosened their hold on the land? In the years of Populism's mounting strength, William Allen White was reaching maturity in Eldorado, Kansas. The children of the few Jews in town mixed freely with the adolescent elite of which White himself was a member, just as Tarkington's Maurice Levy was one of the boys. When White thought of the Jew he thought of the wealth of the tradespeople, of the luxury of their weddings. His own family was well off, and his impressions of his Jewish contemporaries were favorable.

But there were many others who believed "all trade is treachery," who believed that commerce "by the manipulation of Satan" has become "a curse to humanity" dominating all the peoples of the earth. To those people every Jewish storekeeper was in the advance guard of the new civilization and bore the standard of all the dread forces that threatened their security. In those formative years of the 1890s, the injured economic groups of American society had issued the cries of an infant in agony that has no words to express its pain. Searching vainly for the means of relief, they could scarcely guess that the source of their trials was a basic change in the world in which they lived. Groping toward an understanding of that change, some perceived its instrument to be the Jew. If all trade was treachery and Babylon the city, then the Jew—stereotyped, inextricably involved in finance, mysterious—stood ready to be assigned the role of arch-conspirator.

The precipitant factor was the development of a new conception of race. The theory that men were divided into breeds that were biologically different and incapable of fusion ran counter both to the Christian doctrine of the brotherhood of man and to the American ideal of nationality. Though new, the notion nevertheless had important sources of strength in the American environment.

The first denials of human brotherhood came in the South, out of the need of slaveholders for a moral defense of the labor system on which their society rested. The Civil War, which eliminated the old legal basis for differentiation between Negroes and white people, made the necessity more compelling. Constant repetition spread the idea that color was a mark of innate difference, and that the Negro was inherently inferior to the white.

The arguments developed against the Negroes could easily be applied to other groups. Thus, in the succession of crises on the Pacific Coast, the Orientals became the butt of racist opposition; and although white immigrants of many origins were prominently engaged in both the anti-Chinese and the anti-Japanese movements, the same racist doctrine was shortly applied against them.

As the century drew to a close, the complaint was heard that not everyone was equally capable of becoming an American. Prescott Hall and the Immigration Restriction League saw the face of the country changing and did not like what they saw. The new industrialism and monster cities had distorted the old standards, had undermined the old values. Unwilling to recognize the true sources of these changes they blamed the newcomers for lowered rates of wages, for slums, and for corrupt institutions. The restrictionists urged that the United States pick and choose carefully among those who knocked at the gates of the New World. Instead of admitting all indiscriminately, the nation must select the stocks that could best be grafted on to the "original American tree."

After 1900 a determined campaign for the reversal of the traditional American attitude of free immigration gained currency. The campaign shifted its sights from time to time, but its ultimate objective remained the same: the limitation of admission to the United States to people closely similar to the Anglo-Saxon breed that was assumed to be responsible for American well-being and progress.

To show that further immigration was undesirable, the restrictionist had to fly in the face of history; after all, America was the very product of immigration. The proponents of the new policy accomplished this difficult feat of illogic by arguing that the immigrants then applying for admission were different in kind, and inferior to, those who had come earlier. The old immigrants, they mistakenly asserted, were northwestern, blond, Teutonic, Protestant; the new were southeastern, dark, Slavic-Latin, Semitic, and non-Protestant.

The Jews, migrating in large numbers at the turn of the century, were usually included in the general condemnation of the "new" immigrants. Thus William Z. Ripley, a liberal social scientist, shivered at the thought of the flood of Polish-Jewish human beings which threatened to inundate the country. On the other hand, N. S. Shaler, a restrictionist geologist, would have admitted the Jews, since he believed that their "racial traits" of quickness and intelligence would stand the country in good stead.

This division of opinion was indicative of the uncertainty of attitudes toward the Jews. In good faith, a restrictionist in Boston could ask Louis D. Brandeis to join in the anti-immigrant campaign. Whether the new concept of race, clearly intolerant of Latins and Slavs, was also strong enough to break down the old tolerance toward Jews was for the time being a moot question.

Part of the answer came from abroad. European racial thinking, closer to a medieval past, aimed clearly at the Jew who was everywhere in the minority and in some places still not endowed with the full rights of citizenship. All too soon the subtler intellectual expressions of that European prejudice found an audience on this side of the ocean. Three anti-Semitic theorists in particular were attentively read in the United States in the last decade of the century. The work of Ernest Renan had a poetic attraction that coated the prejudices it contained. The writings of the Count Arthur de Gobineau had a spurious appearance of scientific objectivity. And the massive volumes of Houston Stewart Chamberlain seemed to draw upon all the resources of modern scholarship to support their arguments. These were the sources from which perilous misconceptions flowed.

From the works of Renan, Americans learned to think of a "Semitic spirit" constant through the ages, not subject to national and cultural influences and often hostile to them. From Gobineau and from his disciple Vacher de Lapouge, they acquired an acquaintance with the "Aryan" race, the presumed fount, since the origins of modern times, of all the elements of Western civilization. Chamberlain supplied the synthesis; he laid down a scheme that interpreted all of modern history in terms of an elemental conflict between the "Aryan" and the Semite, between the forces of strength and weakness, of idealism and materialism, of nobility and servility.

These ideas were by no means fully absorbed or consciously accepted, but they left definable traces in the minds of thousands of Americans. Meshing with consciousness of color and consciousness of nationality, they helped to produce an American racial ideology.

By the time World War I added its own peculiar complexities to the problem, there was a noticeable though inchoate tendency to think of the Jews as a race apart. Furthermore, that trend had acquired an intellectual frame of reference and a good deal of its vocabulary from the innocent work of sociologists and anthropologists. For these thinkers, in pursuit of their own inquiries, blundered into a line of thought that was a godsend to the racist.

The American sociologists of the first two decades of the twentieth century were drawn to the subject by the necessity of dealing in a concrete way with such questions as poverty, crime, housing, the family, and religion. They tended on the basis of these specific problems to generalize concerning the nature of society and of social institutions. They could not but notice that ethnic factors were important in those questions. Since immigrants and Negroes occupied the worst quarters in the great cities, and held the poorest paying jobs, they were particularly likely to become cases for the social workers and subjects of social pathology.

Too often American social theorists, influenced by all the racist forces that played upon their contemporaries, preferred to see the source of the evil not in their own society but in innate deficiencies in the minority groups which stubbornly refused to allow themselves to be reformed. Not infrequently the sociologists and social workers, who started out to do good for the immigrant, ended up by hating him because the newcomer did not accept the social workers' view of what "good" was.

The ultimate extension of planning in this field appeared to be eugenics; through that science one could plan a whole society in advance by the selection of the proper future parents. Combining the idea of eugenic selection and innate racial qualities, the great majority of American sociologists in the decade after 1910 reached conclusions, disproved by subsequent research, that definitely marked certain ethnic groups, including the Jews, as inferior and unassimilable. In the ranks of those who wrote in this vein were such progressive professors as John R. Commons, Edward A. Ross, and Henry Pratt Fairchild. These men sometimes denied that they were prejudiced, but they wrote and acted as if they were. Their words and deeds were taken as models by thousands influenced by the prestige of academic position and of scientific learning. That the professors thought themselves temperate and cautious was hardly a virtue in the final analysis, for more popular writers threw caution to the winds and gave the same ideas more radical expression.

Thus in 1908 Alfred P. Schultz published a volume called *Race or Mongrel*. The contents were adequately paraphrased in the subtitle: *a Theory that the Fall of Nations is Due to In-*

termarriage with Alien Stocks; . . . a Prophecy that America Will Sink to Early Decay Unless Immigration is Rigorously Restricted. Among the "alien stocks" that threatened "Aryan purity" in the United States were the Jews.

Eight years later the masterpiece of this school, Madison Grant's *The Passing of the Great Race,* saw the light of day. This work, which passed through edition after edition, proved to hundreds of thousands of horrified "Nordic" Americans that the purity of their great race had been contaminated by contact with inferior breeds—among them the Negroes, the Latins, and the Semite Jews—dwarfed in stature, twisted in mentality, and ruthless in the pursuit of their own self-interest.

When these ideas were repeated by Lothrop Stoddard in 1920, from the point of view of the eugenicist, and by B. J. Hendrick in 1924, from the point of view of the historian, they added little that was new to the stock of prejudices. But the popularity of such books illustrated again the continued hold of this brand of racism upon the contemporary mind. In no small measure that hold was due to the fact that these notions passed current as science.

By 1920 a full-fledged racial ideology colored the thinking of many Americans. The conquest of opinion was by no means complete; the traditional American attitude of tolerance still acted as a brake upon the headlong sweep of these new ideas. What was ominous was the support the ideas received from occasional incidents at the practical level.

In practice as in theory, the Jews were not alone singled out. The racist found equally his enemies the Latins, the Slavs, and all the colored peoples. If the Jews were often the first to draw fire, that was because local circumstances and their established place in American society sometimes made them the most prominent targets.

Social mobility was always an important characteristic of the American scheme for living. A great deal of freedom in the economic structure made room for the free play of talents and permitted newcomers to make their way from the lower to the higher rungs in the occupational ladder. In the absence of an hereditary aristocracy, social position generally accompanied economic position. Those who occupied the higher places resented the competition from those who climbed out of the lower places. Already in the 1850s newspapers sometimes carried the injunction over their help-wanted ads, "No Irish Need Apply!"

The earliest encounters of the Jews with this feature of the American social system were like those of other immigrants. In adjusting to the economy, some groups moved upward much more rapidly than others. The Jews were among those who advanced most quickly in earning power and in social position. Their special difficulties arose from this very circumstance: they seemed singularly to rise faster than other peoples of recent foreign origin. All who mounted the economic ladder earned the resentment of the well-established. But persistent stereotypes now set in; racial images gave the rapid climb of the Jews an ominous, mysterious quality, as if these interlopers were a threat to all existing values.

Economic power in America was usually enveloped in symbols of prestige and position—good family, membership in the appropriate churches and associations, residence in select districts, and participation in communal activities. Success by Jews was resented, not only because the success of every new arrival seemed to leave less room for those already entrenched, but also because success in their case was not graced with the proper symbols, did not take the proper form.

Furthermore, the rapidity of the climb heightened the sense of difference between Jews and non-Jews at the upper economic levels. Some Jews reached positions of economic power and influence within a single generation, a time interval not long enough for social adaptation. The contrast in behavior was therefore particularly noticeable and confirmed the impression of the Jew as an outsider. "High society" and its lowlier imitators, uncomfortable at the entrance of any newcomers, in the case of the Jew could ascribe its discomfort to the difference in manners rather than to an inherent unwillingness to make room for competitors. His exceptional mobility and the fear of his strangeness made the Jew the most prominent and the most vulnerable target of all the minorities discriminated against.

Exclusion was first prominently expressed in areas that involved the use of leisure-time facilities, that is, in vacation places, in clubs, and in social groups of various kinds. Such activities, being less formalized than the activities of business or politics, were open to intimate personal contacts, and therefore felt the strangers' presence more sensitively. What is more, these activities involved the whole family. Unlike the office or the workshop, where each man could deal impersonally and almost anonymously with individuals as individuals, the resort or dance drew in the members of his family and made the entrenched member more conscious of the newcomer's background and origin. Toward the end of the nineteenth century, many clubs and societies began consistently to bar Jews from membership.

These social slights ultimately had an effect upon other activities. To the extent that business and political contacts often were made within the realm of the club or society, those who were excluded from the club or society were automatically at a disadvantage in other fields.

Soon that discrimination became more direct. After 1910, as the sons of the immigrant Jews entered more keenly and more noticeably into competition for professional and white-collar places in the American economic system, the weight of prejudice against them became formal and more open. Newspaper advertisements began specifically to exclude Jews from consideration for certain positions. Access to many professions was arbitrarily if informally limited.

Uneasily many Americans accepted this pattern of discrimination. Although not a few were still conscious enough of their heritage of freedom and equality to protest against the tendency, all too many, lulled by the racist justification of ineradicable differences, were disposed to acquiesce. The formation of the Anti-Defamation League of B'nai B'rith in 1913 to fight these trends indicated a growing awareness of the seriousness of the problem.

A sudden eruption, two years later, displayed the ugly turn the forces of racism could take. Appropriately enough the eruption came in the South, the source of so much of the festering venom; and appropriately enough it came in the new, not the old South, in industrial Atlanta rather than on the romantic plantation.

Among the disorganized masses of men thrown together in

the American cities, grievances with no hope of redress from "legal" channels often led to violent outbursts of mob action. Many people did not trust their government, were ready to believe that their police department and courts had sold out to special interests, and, under provocation, were willing to take direct action themselves.

Distinctive minorities were particularly subject to violent reprisals when their actions seemed to run against the cherished patterns of the community, yet involved no clear infraction of the law. The Negroes annually paid their toll to the lynchers. In the 1890s Italians in New Orleans and Irishmen in Boston had suffered the harsh effects of mob violence.

In 1915 the blow fell upon Leo Frank, a Jewish resident of Atlanta, Georgia. Accused of the murder of a fourteen-year-old girl and convicted on the flimsiest grounds, he was taken from jail and lynched the day after the governor of the state had commuted his death sentence to a prison term.

Many factors combined to draw the web of hatred around Frank's neck. He was a Northerner and an employer of labor, and earned a full share of mistrust on those grounds alone. As a Jew he inherited all the dislikes stirred up by the racist writers of the period, and also the murky suspicions about Jewish blood murders left over from agitation of American opinion by such a trumped-up charge in Russia a few years earlier. Finally, the indignation everywhere outside the state that followed Frank's conviction, and the ultimate commutation of the sentence by the governor, raised the suspicion that justice was being frustrated through the intercession of powerful, hostile outsiders. Under skillful manipulation, these became the goads that prodded the mob into action.

The manipulation came from Tom Watson. By 1913 this man had a long political career behind him. A sympathizer with the cause of the poor in his own region, Georgia and the South, he had been prominent as a Populist and as a leader in the progressive movements at the turn of the century. But the years after 1900 were a long series of frustrations not so much in terms of personal ambitions but in terms of the success of the Populist program for which he fought.

In common with many other men of his period, Watson blamed this deterioration upon the interference of outside interests. At first his hostility focused upon the traditional enemy of fundamentalist America, the Roman Catholic Church, and he engaged in a long, bitter campaign of vilification through his journals and books. But in practice as in theory, prejudice was not easily limited to one group. The Frank case offered an alternative target, and Watson transferred the identical arguments he used against the Catholics to the Jews. He rallied his followers with the slogan that Frank must be executed to eliminate outside Jewish interference from Georgia.

In an immediate sense, Watson was successful. Frank died and Watson himself rode to continued political power on the basis of his leadership in the anti-Semitic campaign. Local bitterness raised by the issue persisted for many years. Yet the very violence of the language Watson used, the very barbarousness of the methods of his mob revolted the great mass of Americans outside his state. The rude gallows at Marietta, Georgia, cast a somber shadow across the land, a premonitory warning of what might develop.

Then came the war, and the presence of a genuine external

danger, for a time, seemed to still internal dissensions. Jews contributed with their fellow citizens to the winning of the struggle, and their participation was officially recognized by the government through such agencies as the Jewish Welfare Board. Moreover, the very slogans in terms of which the war was fought rebuked and chastened those who promoted intolerance at home.

If the war brought peace, the peace unloosed the bitter passions of disappointment and betrayal. The outcome of the conflict was so different from the stated aims, for the sake of which so many sacrifices had been made, that millions of Americans, feeling cheated, turned against the aims themselves. In the five years after the armistice, the United States seemed to wish to draw back into a chauvinistic isolation, to cut its ties with the rest of the world, and to forget not only the phrases but also the ideals that had sparked the war effort. Rejection of the League of Nations and the World Court, and the development of a high tariff system were surface indications of the deep undertow of fear.

Dangers from abroad threatened the nation. From every quarter of the outside world, the fearful saw the menace of subversion. Xenophobia seeped into all the corners of life in the United States; and all too many gullible Americans were now prepared to associate the Jews with those threats.

Revolution in Russia brought terror to the heart. Was this the first of the great uprisings of which Jack London and Ignatius Donnelly had written, in which an underworld of godless anarchy would rise up to destroy the world of existing values? Main Street hastened to defend itself, clamped down on signs of dissidence, and examined every trace of the foreign with distrust. Patriotic societies in New York demanded legislation to outlaw the speaking on the public streets of any language but English; and a Senate committee heard charges that East Side Jews had caused the Bolshevik Revolution.

Paradoxically, many 100-per-cent Americans turned for an explanation to an evil little volume imported from abroad. *The Protocols of the Elders of Zion* was an obvious forgery, earlier concocted by the Czar's secret police. It purported to record the proceedings, in Prague, of a secret body, plotting by means of the gold standard to capture the world on behalf of international Jewry. This flimsy story, so clearly fraudulent on the face of it, passed through edition after edition, and found credence among thousands of well-intentioned, if uncritical, Americans who lived in a world in which truth was not separate from fiction and in which the idealistic promises of the war had led to betrayal. Among the credulous was Henry Ford, who gave the support of his reputation and the columns of his *Dearborn Independent* to these slanders.

The most flamboyant preachers of 100-per-cent Americanism were the members of the latter-day Ku Klux Klan. This obscure organization had started in the South shortly before World War I. It assumed the title of the old Reconstruction bands, made popular by a film that had just swept the country, D. W. Griffith's *Birth of a Nation*. The new Klan operated first as a simple racket, fleecing the joiners through a fancy price on sheet-uniforms. But between 1920 and 1925 the Klan grew in numbers and spread out geographically until it attained a membership of close to four million, heavily concentrated in the North, particularly in the states of Oregon, Ohio, Indiana, and Illinois.

The Klan found its leading antagonist in the Pope, and thus fell into the tradition of confusing issues by identifying Catholicism with internationalism. But it had hatred enough left over for the Jews, also supposedly contaminated by international affiliations, and for the Negroes, who were vulnerable enough without any such pretext.

After 1925 the strength of the Klan ebbed away. In the next few years people, no matter how insecure, were no longer likely to phrase their fears in terms of an international menace to the United States. For a while, it appeared that disarmament treaties and the Kellogg Pact had made the nation safe against attack from without; prosperity kept it safe against attack from within.

The one permanent result of the postwar fright had been the final reversal, between 1920 and 1924, of the historic American immigration policy. The legislation of those years not only cut drastically the number of new entrants, but did so in terms of a crude racist philosophy that set up standards of desirability for all the peoples of the world, counting some high, some low, almost exactly as Madison Grant and Prescott Hall had counseled.

The consequences for the American social and economic system was drastic. With no more newcomers, economic expansion slackened, and before long there was a noticeable contraction in the range of opportunities. Between 1920 and 1940, for instance, the number of practitioners in such professions as medicine and engineering remained almost stationary. That meant that competition for the desirable places became sharper than ever. If the number of doctors did not grow, every new Jewish doctor deprived the son of a gentile of his place. Discriminatory practices moved into the open; the Kings County Hospital fracas in 1927 revealed the extent to which anti-Semitism had been accepted in a public institution serving a community largely Jewish.

In the 1920s almost every leading American college and university, formally or informally, adopted a quota system for Jewish students. Unofficial regulatory agencies made difficult the way into almost every profession. By 1940 representative groups in the fields of dentistry and psychiatry were going so far as to propose openly a quota system in those fields. Everywhere the difficulty of securing desirable employment became constantly more oppressive.

In those years, too, the pattern of exclusion extended into the field of housing. Whole areas of many cities, through voluntary covenants of real-estate owners, were abruptly closed to persons of "Hebrew descent."

While these effects were still being felt, the depression after 1929 struck a blow at the stability of the American economy from which there was no recovery for almost a decade. Through the 1930s close to ten million unemployed men and their families lived by the insecure margin of public relief or of charity, and remained the prey of all sorts of demagogues ready to capitalize upon their fears.

One impulse that focused the revived hatreds upon the Jews came from Germany. The advent of the Nazis to power had a double effect. It upset the stability of Europe and of the world and revived American fears of involvement in foreign quarrels. More directly, the accession of the National Socialists to power gave control of a sovereign government to a group aggressively interested in spreading anti-Semitic ideas throughout the world.

Hitler's primary agents in this mission in the United States were German-Americans, rigidly organized. Large numbers of Germans, many of them veterans of the Kaiser's army still imbued with national pride, had entered the United States in the 1920s under the quota laws which had granted the Germans a high percentage of immigration places.

Some of these people had been early joiners in such patriotic societies as the Teutonia, but these groups had been small in number and short of purse. After 1932 however, they had the support of agencies of the German government, from which they secured organizational leadership, funds, and a steady stream of propaganda to be spread throughout the United States.

Many German-Americans were first drawn to these societies through simple fraternal and nationalistic motives. But as the German government plunged ever deeper down the path of anti-Semitism, to the horror of the rest of the civilized world, defense of Germany tended to become defense of anti-Semitism. Before long the only way to uphold the good name of the Fatherland was to convince others that the Nazi persecution of the Jews was necessary to save Western civilization from the menace of world Jewry.

Hitler had not been in power for a year when the American societies were reorganized and centralized in the Friends of the New Germany, later known as the German-American Bund. Under the successive leadership of Heinz Spanknoebel, Fritz Gissibl, Fritz Kuhn, and Wilhelm Kunze, the Bund set itself the task of popularizing the doctrines of Hitler's new order. Newspapers and books, inspired from abroad, gave new life to the stock libels about the Jews. Camps maintained the morale of the members, and public meetings served to infect outsiders.

A great part of the early financial support for these activities came from the German government. In this respect, the Bund was a Nazi agency. In furthering Hitlerite objectives, it performed, on the direct operational level, the same function being performed, on a more respectable level, by such native-born apologists as George Sylvester Viereck and by the Flanders Hall publishing house.

Unfortunately, Hitler did not have to rely exclusively upon Germans to do his work in the United States. Native tools, working for their own interests, also served his purposes.

Among the insecure groups rendered more insecure by the depression were millions of men of varying backgrounds ready to be enlisted in a crusade, men awaiting some clear call to salvation. More than anything else they wanted something about which they could be enthusiastic, some cause in which they could believe and which would bring the promise of security. Out of such cravings came the support for all sorts of new movements untouched by any trace of anti-Semitism, the Townsend Plan, for example, or EPIC (End Poverty in California). The vast majority who participated in such drives did not follow bigoted leaders, but rather labored to attain their economic ends without group hatred. Yet in this inchoate mass of distressed people, a small proportion responded to appeals that were clearly fascist in nature and that were often oriented around anti-Semitic programs. Between 1933 and 1939 some hundred organizations, large and small, drew together the Jew-haters into a potentially dangerous force.

There was no consistency to these groups, except their common confusion and inconsistency. While all were insecure, the sources of their insecurity were diverse. Some, for instance, carried on in the spirit of the 1920s; these were chauvinists, foes of the "international" Jew, striving for purity of the American race, hostile to anything alien. Such people were most numerous in the South and Middle West, the old Klan territory. They were Protestants, often fundamentalist in religion, and terrified at the disappearance of an American way of life that had never existed. They joined William Dudley Pelley's Silver Shirts and the revived Klan, or became the audience of Gerald L. K. Smith and Gerald Winrod.

Another fund of discontent was different in origin but similar in expression. The Catholics, particularly of the second and third generations, had the same economic difficulties as other marginal groups in the 1930s, and emerged with the same feelings of insecurity, the same longing for a panacea. The Catholics themselves had had a long history of experience with bigotry in the United States, and had reasons in plenty for distrusting this aspect of the American spirit. Nevertheless, anti-Semitism made some headway among them.

Father Charles E. Coughlin had gained an enormous radio audience before 1936 by focusing his sermons on economic questions and by support of the New Deal. Shortly after his break with President Roosevelt, he used his radio time and the columns of his newspaper, *Social Justice*, to attack the Jews. His stock in trade was old and shopworn: the international plot of Communists and bankers to hand over the world to the

Jews. In 1938 Father Coughlin's followers gathered into organizations which subsequently became the Christian Front.
Among the leadership was Father Curran, often referred to as
"Father Coughlin's Eastern Representative," John F. Cassidy,
and Francis P. Moran. The Christian Front spread the current
anti-Semitic propaganda, and also held provocative meetings.

The diversity of the sources from which these anti-Semitic
groups sprang accounted for the fact that they were never able
to unite, to eliminate conflicts among rival leaders, or to pool
interests and support. Some of these organizations attracted
substantial financial backing from time to time, but they never
found a basis of cooperation and their achievements were neg-
ligible.

Furthermore their impact on politics was only transitory.
In the years before Pearl Harbor there was an unprecedented
willingness to raise the Jewish issue as such, in reference to
international affairs. As the prospect of war became more real,
month after month in 1941, many well-meaning people, committed to keeping the country neutral, succumbed to the temptation of ascribing to the Jews the responsibility for the nation's foreign policy. Men as well known and respected as
Charles A. Lindbergh and Senator Gerald P. Nye expressed
themselves in terms that created doubts as to their motivations.
It had been shocking in 1933 to hear Congressman MacFadden
of Pennsylvania use the halls of the Capitol as a sounding board
for anti-Semitic charges. Eight years later, not long before
Pearl Harbor, it was commonplace to find Congressmen Thor-
kelson and Rankin, in the boldest terms, ascribing American
participation in the war of 1941 to nefarious Jewish influences.

Yet the war, and the horrible results of anti-Semitism it revealed, stifled Hitler's American imitators. The little native *führers* were ultimately exposed as allies of the national enemies, and the revelation of what had transpired in the concentration camps sickened the American people and turned them away from the doctrines associated with Dachau and Buchenwald.

After the end of the war, efforts to revive anti-Semitism by such groups as the Columbians in South Carolina collapsed ignominiously. Gerald Smith wandered drearily unheard through the land, and the wild accusations of Professor John O. Beaty of Southern Methodist University and of California State Senator Jack B. Tenney earned the credence only of a lunatic fringe in the unstable areas of the country. The test came after 1948. Although a handful of Jews were uncovered among the Communist conspirators—enough to provide the anti-Semitic hate groups with some ammunition—no serious effort was made to connect the Jews as a group with communism. There was not the least reluctance to put direction of the whole atomic-energy program in the hands of a Jew, Lewis L. Strauss.

The more permanent consequence of all the racial agitation was upon the Jews themselves. The shocking realization that their place in American society was being questioned affected their continuing adjustment to American conditions. Coming as it did in decades unsettled by depression and war, the strain of struggle against anti-Semitism consumed much of the group's energy and left a significant impress upon a still uncertain future. Long after the crisis passed, twinges of doubt would recur. Were they really safely at home in the United States?

Abraham Cahan (right), a towering figure in Yiddish journalism,
emigrated from Russia in 1882 and
died in 1951. (Courtesy of *Jewish
Daily Forward*.) . . . Samuel Gompers (below, right), for many years
President of the American Federation of Labor, came to New York
from England in 1863. (Courtesy
of *Jewish Daily Forward*.) . . .
Jacob Schiff, raised in a Frankfurt
ghetto, became famous as a finan-
cier and philanthropist. (From
Harpers Weekly, October, 1890.)

Two Jewish comedians of different American eras and traditions: Sigmund Mogaliesco of the late nineteenth-century Yiddish stage, and the versatile Danny Kaye. (Wide World Photo.)

CHAPTER NINE

The Reordering of Jewish
Communal Life: 1920–1954

Those who lived through the years of the virulent spread of anti-Semitism could not have known that the fever would ultimately be quieted. The persistence of attacks upon the American Jews came to dominate their thoughts and activities. These attacks impelled the Jews to create the means of self-defense and rendered the idea of a Zionist refuge more attractive than before. As the crisis grew more intense in the 1930s, it exacerbated the old problems of communal organization and forced a reexamination of what it meant to be a Jew in American society. Only after a second world war, when the fire of the old hatreds died down, were the Jews freed of the necessity of standing always on guard. They were then able to turn their energies to adjusting to the new social situation in the United States.

In the 1920s the necessities of defense against anti-Semitism were paramount. The violence of the unprovoked attacks upon the group left no alternative. The Klan and its imitators had no interest in abstract discussion. The threat they posed was immediate.

Yet in that decade resistance by the Jews exuded the confidence of moderation. They felt reassured as they surveyed the past and took stock of the long American tradition of tolerance that their "crackpot" foes would never gain substantial followings. Even the millions of Klansmen could be explained away—albeit uneasily—as eccentric representatives of the booboisie who roused the mirth of all intelligent men.

The laughter turned hollow in the 1930s when another such eccentric demonstrated how a modern state could be turned to the brutal service of a racial ideology. As time made gradually clear the meaning of the news from Germany, the Jews of America became thoroughly dismayed. The Nazis chose as victims the most cultured and well-integrated sector of modern Jewry; they thereby destroyed the argument that the Jews had only to cast off their differences to dissipate prejudice. Furthermore, the brutalities unleashed by the fascists were not the primitive products of the religious rage of Russian *pogromchiks*. These were calculated, scientific measures, using racial hatreds manufactured by propaganda for political ends. To many Jews, the ineluctable question became: if it could happen there, why not in the United States? That thought imparted a sense of high urgency to the determination to resist. For a quarter of a century after 1920, the American Jewish group devoted its most serious thoughts to the meaning of the struggle against racism.

At first the battle against discrimination had rested upon the tactics of intercession, the appeal to the favor of the influential. This was simply the extension of the traditional means by which, for centuries, the Jews had courted the good will or capitalized upon the cupidity of princes to secure the privilege of existence. Now, too, American Jews sought by private intercession and unofficial representations to secure the alleviation of discriminatory conditions. Thus, if a corporation's help-wanted advertisements specified, "Protestants only," a substantial Jewish stockholder might tactfully suggest to the president that the personnel manager was acting unwisely.

In the United States, however, prejudice was not altogether a private matter. Democracy made the difference, for private views, widely held, were transmuted into public policy. Furthermore, in a democracy there was no appeal to a prince; the people went their own way. Only education and understanding could direct the way they went.

Through the 1920s the effort to give Americans a better comprehension of the problem had been mostly through apologetics. Jews attempted by a display of their contributions to the country's welfare to prove that they had earned a place in American society. The output of books, pamphlets, orations, and pageantry, directed to that end, did not slacken in the 1930s, but other methods also received attention. Increasingly, there were efforts to comprehend the sources of prejudice scientifically and, by diffusing information, to dispel some of the dark shadows from which the hatreds sprang.

As the crisis deepened after 1930, neither intercession nor education proved adequate; Hitler's coming to power emphasized the urgency for more aggressive techniques. American Jews began to shift to a more positive stance, seeking more direct and effective means of preventing the growth of fascism and of the anti-Semitism associated with it.

The New Deal showed how political action could further those ends. A large preponderance of American Jews were drawn to Franklin Roosevelt's support. Laborers and shopkeepers, they had been badly hurt by the depression and were attracted by a program that promised economic relief. Furthermore, the Jews as a group were now among the least secure elements, socially and psychologically, in American society, and they valued the assurance of their rights and freedoms implicit in the New Deal ideology of the common man. The fact that such Jews as Samuel I. Rosenman, Benjamin V. Cohen, and Felix Frankfurter were close to the President influenced the shaping of that ideology and also created confidence among Jews as to the good intentions of the government toward them.

The Jews now discovered they were, in the United States, but one of several "minorities," that is, groups regarding themselves as underprivileged. The Negroes, the American Indians, the Italians, the Irish, the Catholics, each felt aggrieved by exclusion from or restriction of opportunities open to other Americans. Combined, all these people became a majority capable of asserting a strong claim to equality. The readiness of the New Dealers to legislate in economic and social matters raised the hope that action by the state might protect the minorities against discrimination. By the end of the 1930s the tactics of Jewish defense had been completely transformed. The Jews no longer imagined their interests to lie in appeals to the powerful but in solidarity with the underprivileged. They sought security not in acts of tolerance for themselves alone but in the general assertion of the rights of all Americans.

The development of this attitude helped prevent the anti-Semitic agitators of the 1930s from coalescing or consolidating their movements. Furthermore, the heartening New Deal concepts of minority rights prepared the way for the positive action of the war years. The outbreak of fighting in 1941, in which all men were asked equally to participate, was the signal for a new effort to assure all of them equal rights. As Jews shared with their fellow citizens the discomforts of the barracks and the dangers of the battlefields, their comradeship made the old prejudices obsolete. Furthermore, the character of the enemy helped to define the issue; it was hard to defend discriminatory practices even faintly analogous to those of the Germans. From 1941 onward there was steady improvement of the status of all the minorities, generally in a direction defined under the New Deal.

Along with the other minorities, the Jews profited. Organized anti-Semitism dropped off rapidly. Acts for fair employment and for nondiscriminatory educational policies in several states noticeably improved their occupational and social prospects. Meanwhile the manpower shortages rendered many such discriminatory devices anachronistic and laid the groundwork for a tolerant reception of the new legislation. After the end of the war, the abatement of anti-Semitic sentiments and practices continued. It seemed certain that the long period—almost a half-century—of trial was over.

Yet the extended crisis and the years of tension had left a great troubling question mark after all the assumptions that Jews could somehow adjust permanently and finally to life in the United States. The doubts once raised could not easily be quieted. Men would not readily lay aside the means of self-defense they had prepared in the years when anti-Semitism was a direct threat. Nor could they immediately shed the modes of thought developed under the pressure of attack.

Largely because of their growing anxieties about their own

future in the United States, the majority of American Jews found themselves, between 1917 and 1945, drawn to support the effort to establish a Jewish homeland in Palestine. They did so not out of the expectation that they might themselves sometimes leave the United States, nor out of conscious adherence to the Zionist ideology that denied the possibility of a sound Jewish life in exile. Rather they were moved by developing events to a vague and inchoate commitment that solution of the Jewish problem could come only by this means.

This commitment had begun to manifest itself just after World War I. Americans had then been elevated to the leadership of world Jewry and had played a prominent part in the peace conferences. The Balfour Declaration and the mandate made some sort of Jewish homeland in Palestine a reality. At the same time, unsettled conditions in Europe and the closing of the American gates left hundreds of thousands of European Jews, with whom the recent American immigrants had close familial ties, anxious to move but with no place to go. The number of Americans who showed their adherence to the Zionist program by purchasing a shekel—the token that enabled them to vote in the organization's elections—mounted from the twenty thousand in 1914 to one hundred and seventy thousand in 1920. Even the reform Central Conference of American Rabbis, though still opposed to a Jewish state, in 1918 came out in favor of immigration to Palestine on the grounds that "Jewish people are, and of right ought to be, at home in all lands." Growth of American Zionist sentiment was steady in the 1920s, marked by revival of interest in the Hebrew language and by participation in the social and economic development of Palestine.

The excited emotions of the period after World War I added strength to the Zionist movement in America. As in the case of other immigrant groups, political nationalism offered a temporary release from the fears and frustrations of postwar adjustment. Here was a way of escaping from the harshness of contact with strangers, a way of finding security in affiliation with the ethnic group, yet a way that was acceptable in terms of the standards of the larger society. The Jews behaved as the Irish and Germans had earlier; feeling rejected by the 100-per-cent Americans, they resorted to a similar nationalism of their own.

Zionism was the outlet, particularly for the second-generation Jews. This group was especially perplexed, as all second generations were, by the question of their place in American culture, confused by specific problems of social and economic adjustment and anxious over the meaning of anti-Semitism. Americans tended to be extremists in the world Zionist movement, in no small measure because they carried into it the whole burden of their worries and fears as American Jews.

Several forces also drew into the movement men who were not nationalists and who earlier had been indifferent to Zionism. Louis D. Brandeis had already had a distinguished career as a lawyer when he joined the Zionist organization in 1912. He would go on to occupy a seat on the highest court in the United States, and also to be president of the movement. Always he had thought his law cases through to the details, crowded his briefs with facts and figures, shunned the delusive abstraction. Experience had taught him also the curse of bigness, the advantages of the small effective unit. Now his eager mind leaped ahead to the potentiality of social experiment in Palestine on a small scale. Here there might be put experimentally into practice the progressive social ideas for which he had fought since 1900. After a time he found the Zionist leaders were not in sympathy with his own ideas, and he withdrew from the active management of affairs. But all his life he retained faith in his vision.

Others, like Jacob Schiff, had at first resisted the Zionist movement, but then saw the future of Palestine as a cultural homeland and wanted "Zion without any 'ism' " as a center from which the whole world could draw spiritual nourishment.

And then there were some American Jews, like Benjamin Cardozo, also to be a member of the Supreme Court, who never accepted the nationalistic implications of Zionism and yet who came now to support it, because not to do so was to oppose it, and therefore to oppose Jews the world over. It was almost as if rising anti-Semitism in the 1920s aligned all men into the ranks of friends or foes, with no middle ground at all.

By the end of the 1920s non-Zionists had evolved a formula by which they could assist the settlements in Palestine through the Jewish Agency. Thereafter, as British intransigence blocked further development of the land under the status quo, American Jews were pushed toward a position in which they had no alternative but to support the Zionists.

Hitlerism, however, was the final and decisive factor. Against the open determination to exterminate the Jews of Europe there seemed no other defense or solution. Nazism made homeless enormous numbers of refugees. American Jews sympathized. But they feared to provoke the anti-Semites by the demand—futile in any case—for relaxation of their country's restrictive immigration policy. Incapable, therefore, of welcoming more than a few of the fugitives, the Jews of the United States thought it wiser to press for resettlement of the victims of Hitlerism in Palestine.

The shock of discovering how small a proportion of Europe's Jews actually survived the decade of fanaticism and war made the task of rescuing the remnant all the more imperative. These developments induced the Jewish labor movement in America to espouse Zionism, pushed the reform wing of Judaism into a position of official neutrality and unofficial support, and strengthened orthodox approval. After 1945 American Jews stood almost solidly behind the Zionists. Only a relatively small group in the American Council for Judaism thereafter remained apart.

The growing preoccupation with Zionism and the simultaneous concern with defense against anti-Semitism significantly influenced the structure of Jewish communal life after 1920. The older patterns of institutional organization persisted, but they could not evade the necessity of adaptation to the interests that now dominated the thoughts of American Jews. Those interests now seemed to demand that the anarchic multiplication of associations yield to a planned, efficient distribution of communal resources. Yet the efforts in that direction invariably stumbled over the difficulty of deciding who would plan, and to what end.

In the decade after the end of World War I, the number of philanthropic, benevolent, and social agencies continued to grow; needs unsatisfied from the past were still being filled. But some of the problems promised to become simpler as immigration declined and finally ended after 1925. It was probable then that the existing institutions would be able to stabilize their services and move into a period of consolidation and internal development.

There was, indeed, considerable improvement in the caliber of the hospitals, homes, orphanages, and other organizations. Anxious to justify themselves by comparison with other public and private institutions, Jews strained every resource in order to keep pace with the latest techniques. The scientific skills of experts replaced the haphazard methods of devoted but incompetent amateur administrators. Obsolete buildings converted from some other use or long since outgrown gave way to imposing new edifices.

Such improvements cost money. Budgets mounted rapidly under the pressure of new expenses. For the time being the necessary sums were available; the spread of federations, the use of more effective modes of fund raising, and the rising income level of various Jewish groups pushed the total raised consistently higher.

The 1930s, however, brought difficult times. The depression hit potential contributors hard, and dwindling receipts reflected their loss of income. Meanwhile, the philanthropies had to compete for funds with skyrocketing demands for defense against discrimination and for Jewish needs overseas. In many communities the burden of financing so many causes led donors to reconsider the nature of the diverse activities they supported. The power of the federations to allocate funds gave them some measure of control over local institutions; and creation of the Council of Jewish Federations and Welfare Funds in 1932 put at their disposal a national instrument for coordinated planning. But the defense and overseas-relief organizations, the obligations of which were rising most rapidly, were out of reach of the federations.

Three national agencies devoted themselves to defense work after 1920, the Anti-Defamation League, the American Jewish Committee, and the American Jewish Congress. The last-named was an outgrowth of the temporary organization created during World War I. Rabbi Stephen S. Wise had refused to acknowledge that this was no more than the *ad hoc* instrument of a specific purpose. He hoped rather that it would continue to exist and would ultimately constitute a general authority over Jewish life in the United States. At a rump meeting after the original Congress had passed out of existence, a group of like-minded individuals assumed the old name and proceeded to act under it, although with a form, and in a spirit, quite different from that which had animated the original organization.

A typical product of the American 1920s, the Congress was imbued with the spirit of Jewish nationalism. The Jews, it asserted, shared not only religion, but "peoplehood," and the Congress was the representative body speaking for them. Since "world Jewry," in their opinion, needed representation in the same way, although on another scale, those who now controlled the Congress in due course created a World Jewish Congress—a supernational integrating body to coordinate the activities of Jews everywhere.

Down to the middle of the 1930s, the American Jewish Congress did not absorb the loyalty of a very large portion of the Jews of the United States. It certainly was never able to play the role in the life of the Jewish communities that its organizers had envisioned. The Congress, like every other voluntary association, was capable of controlling only its own membership and found itself speaking simply for those who adhered to its position. It did not become a body representative of all American Jews, but one that functioned much like its rival agencies.

The American Jewish Congress gained strength from the strain of the 1930s. The events in Europe and in America seemed to support its contention that the Jews were a people apart. The growth of Zionism also helped, for the Congress had early taken an unequivocal stand on the question and its leader, Rabbi Wise, had worked unremittingly for Palestine long before Hitler. Above all, the terms in which Zionism was promoted prepared adherents for the nationalist viewpoint of the Congress.

On problems of defense against discrimination, the Congress also seemed more in accord with the temper of the depression decade. Wise's diffuse liberalism gave him numerous points of contact with the New Deal, and the Congress moved venturesomely to support new legislative proposals that affected minorities and social policy generally. In international affairs it called quickly for retaliation against Hitlerism, and it dabbled in the politics of the United Front.

Yet, though it grew steadily in influence through the 1930s, the Congress came no closer to being a body representative of all American Jews. Indeed, it was now compelled further to share the field with the Jewish Labor Committee, created in 1933. And, in some cities, community councils, organized locally, began also to participate in similar endeavors.

Somewhat the same disorder existed in the administration of

overseas relief. Numerous political groups, interested in the future of Palestine, carried on their own educational and, often, fund-raising programs—the orthodox conservative Mizrachi, the moderate general Zionists, the socialist Poale Zion, and others. In addition, a complex of economic and cultural organizations carried on their own drives. In 1927 some, but not all, of the appeals for funds were federated in the United Palestine Appeal.

The relief programs for Jews outside Palestine remained entirely uncoordinated. Some agencies, like the Hebrew Immigrant Aid Society (HIAS), had originated to meet the earlier problems of immigration. The Joint Distribution Committee, among others, dated back to World War I. And several bodies labored from the 1920s onward for the relief and retraining of Europeans in the Old World and in the New. The problems of the refugees from Hitlerism after 1933 created still other organizations.

In time some of the organizations, not theretofore coordinated, drew together for fund raising. The outbreak of war in 1939 revealed the dangers and crying needs of the future and gave weight to the arguments for unity. The United Jewish Appeal after that year conducted annual campaigns on behalf of the leading overseas agencies. So, too, the American Jewish Committee and the Anti-Defamation League united in fund raising in the Joint Defense Appeal. Finally, in almost all major cities, the United Jewish Appeal, the Joint Defense Appeal, and the local philanthropies combined in a single annual drive. By then the logic of federation had, in many cities, been pushed to its extreme: each Jew made a single donation allocated for him by a hierarchy of intermediaries to the constituent agencies of whose existence the donor was hardly conscious.

These tactical measures, however, simply lumped one budget with another. They did not touch the internal organization of the constituent bodies, which set their own limits as to their ability to coordinate activities. The situation was tolerable as long as the totals collected continued to rise during the war and immediately after. But a reckoning was inevitable if declining incomes should make cutbacks necessary. Yet every experience since 1920 showed it was improbable the Jews would dispense with any of these agencies. There followed, therefore, through the 1940s a worried search for methods of economizing.

One way was to go beyond federation to control the individual agencies by planning. As it was, the multitude of claims was extremely perplexing. The conscientious men of wealth who supported all these activities felt the obligation to give freely, yet they were troubled by the weight of the burden and by doubts as to the proper distribution of their funds. Rarely did they enjoy the self-confidence and familiarity with Judaism and Jewish philanthropies of the generation of Schiff and Marshall. They were more likely to seek the advice of technical experts than to take the risk of independent decision.

Impatient with the apparent disorder of spontaneous voluntary bodies, they were attracted by the concept of a centralizing authority as the source of efficiency. To both the businessman, who understood the advantages of "management" in his own operations, and the reformer, who had no doubt but that disorder could be planned out of human life, social engineering became the magic wand to wave away all difficulties.

Those troubled by the inefficiency of Jewish organizations were joined in their objections by a quite dissimilar group, the rabbis who resented the secular control of Jewish communal life. Laymen, amateurs as it were, had far more power in the determination of events than the clergy. Each rabbi in his own congregation was subject to the expressed needs and opinions of his trustees, and in most welfare and communal associations and institutions his voice was hardly heeded at all. Therefore he often longed for some centralized organization that would restrain the inclination of any Jewish body to run off at the whim of its own leadership. Certainly the rabbinate would be more influential working as a group through such an organization.

The rising nationalist sentiment of the period added support to the general demand for unity. Those who thought of "Jewish peoplehood" as a living force wished to see that people endowed with political attributes, in the United States as well as Palestine. Thus the Zionists labored to create a unified community in the United States in order to support the Jewish state of the future both materially and through influence on the American government. Similarly, non-Zionist nationalists, thinking along eastern European lines, regarded a centralized authority as a necessity to Jewish survival.

Finally, the impulse toward centralization elicited a very general response even from those removed from the organized communal concerns. The years since 1920 had spread a worrisome sense of insecurity through many American ethnic groups. Social changes of unparalleled magnitude threatened every semblance of security. To the Jews, whether affiliated or not, the rise of organized anti-Semitism at home and abroad was shocking; the enormous dislocations of place and of status through which many passed in the course of a lifetime were equally disturbing; and rapid alterations in the social environment deprived them of the fixed points by which to judge themselves in relation to others. Under these circumstances, some of the fearful lost confidence in the voluntary organizations and wondered whether Jews really could develop an integrated life in the United States with no more protection than these loose spontaneous societies afforded.

It was in unity alone that one could find the necessary strength to face the threatening world; hence the hope that some large, authoritative, powerful body might emerge to stand between the individual and his potential enemies in other groups, a body strong enough to impose discipline within its own ranks and to stand up against the hostile forces outside them.

The longing for unity grew more intense in the 1940s as the war drew to a close. The possible analogy with the postwar crisis of 1918 led men to speculate about the problems of the coming peace. Would not a depression follow the halt in the production of munitions and bring with it renewed unemployment and anti-Semitism? Would not the Jews of Europe need as much relief as formerly? If so, the American Jews would be called upon for unprecedented financial, political, and diplomatic efforts. The anticipated pressures induced many Jews to seek some form of cooperation among their competing organizations.

The renewed efforts toward unity stemmed in part from the conviction of Henry Monsky, president of B'nai B'rith, that some extraordinary "united Jewish front" was essential to

Caricatures from without and within. Above, from *Puck*, March 22, 1895, and below from *Yiddish Puck*, November 28, 1894. The Yiddish caption reads: *Worker*: "Only 50 cents for the lot! You advertise you make loans at full worth!" *Pawnbroker*: "Full worth to me!"

GOING TOO FAR.

Mr. Ochsenheimer (angrily). — I vill speak to der Rabbi about dit.
Mrs. Ochsenheimer. — Aboudt vot?
Mr. Ochsenheimer. — Vy, dem Cohen Broders, der pawnbrokers, adfertisin' dere pawnaws right in der Synagogue!

אין פאאינשאפ.

ארבייטער. (אין פאאינשאפ) דיא אלע גענענשטענדיע קאסטען מיר צעהן דאלאר און איהר גיט מיר פאר זיי בלויז 50 סענט. האם איהר אליין גיט נים גענעלדעם אין דיא צייטונגען, אז איהר לייהעט אויף יעדער זאך דאס גאנצע געלד פון איהר ווערמה?

פאאונברא꞉קער. איך האב דאמים גמיינט דעם ווערמה וואם עס האם עס פאר מיר...

Louis D. Brandeis (top, left), Justice of the United States Supreme Court, 1916–1939 (Courtesy of American Jewish Archives); Benjamin N. Cardozo (top, right), Justice of the United States Supreme Court, 1932–1938 (Courtesy of Wide World Studio); Louis Marshall (below, left), distinguished lawyer and founder of the American Jewish Committee in 1906 (Courtesy of Library of Jewish Information); Rabbi Stephen S. Wise of New York, an ardent proponent of Zionism.

cope with the calamitous problems posed by World War II. In 1943 he invited some thirty-five associations to assemble in Pittsburgh to consider the postwar status of the Jews. Thirty-two of the invited groups met and issued a call for an American Jewish Assembly that would devise a concrete program and choose representatives to implement it in cooperation with delegates of Jews from other parts of the world.

The American Jewish Committee refused at first to participate in this project. It believed in voluntary cooperation among autonomous agencies, but not in unification under majority rule. It objected "to any plan that . . . set up the Jews as a separate political enclave"; and the Assembly appeared, in structure and purpose, to do just that. As an alternative, the Committee proposed a conference of groups representing various points of view "to find what areas of agreement exist that ought to constitute a common ground for united action. Such a conference would not make any claim to speak on behalf of the totality of American Jews; it would not attempt to bind or coerce its own minorities."

Far-reaching concessions apparently met the Committee's objections, including a change in the name of the proposed organization from Assembly to Conference. Yet even before the first sessions in August, 1943, there were indications that these assurances were not literally intended by all the participants. Some individuals harbored more ambitious second thoughts. "Officially the Conference will gather for the limited purpose of agreeing on a program of postwar Jewish demands," the *Congress Weekly* acknowledged. But, it went on to say, "Unofficially it is the historic destiny of the Conference to become the promoter of Jewish thoughts and consciousness." The Conference was to be an "organization in which the collective responsibility of American Israel" would find expression.

The contradictory assumptions of the participants pulled the Conference down to a speedy and ignominious collapse. On the first consequential test, the majority resorted to the tactics of the political steamroller and forced through to adoption a resolution repugnant to the minority. Again the victory only exposed the futility of such tactics. Those who won the vote simply forced the minority to withdraw and thereby destroyed the structure of the whole organization. As an alternative, the most important defense agencies in 1944 founded the National Community Relations Advisory Council to "serve as a coordinating and clearance agency," seeking areas of agreement among organizations which had already clearly demonstrated their unwillingness to be unified. The NCRAC functioned effectively through the rest of the decade.

Meanwhile American Jews shouldered world-wide burdens of unprecedented magnitude. The settlements in Palestine required continuing aid, and the shattered communities of Europe were desperately in need of rescue. There were few corners of the earth to which the fugitives from Hitlerism could flee. To many Americans it seemed the only feasible solution was migration of the uprooted to the Holy Land, where alone they were welcome.

The uncompromising attitude of the British Government stood in the way. The Biltmore Program of 1942 had committed the official Zionists to the creation of a "Jewish Commonwealth" in Palestine. Yet a great many Americans would have been satisfied with less than an independent state, if only the way were open to settlement there of some of the refugees. Precisely on that point the British Government was most obstinate. It held to the restrictive policy of the White Paper of 1939, which severely limited the admission of Jews, thus pushing Americans into a position which left no alternative but support of the Zionists.

The struggle over the future of Palestine waited for the end of the war against Germany and Japan. Thereafter no accommodation was possible between the ambitions of the Zionists and the imperial plans of the British. The impasse finally led to the withdrawal of the English and the open warfare of Jews and Arabs by which Israel established its independence. A few Americans enlisted in the ranks of the fighting men. Many more contributed the money to finance the struggle. And political pressure on the administration in Washington kept it friendly to the new nation.

The creation of the State of Israel aroused widespread enthusiasm among the Jews of the United States, an enthusiasm reflected in the increase of donations to the United Jewish Appeal to well over the $150,000,000 mark, a level of giving that could not be long maintained. The fall in contributions after 1948 revived projects for centralizing and unifying various aspects of communal life, but with little more success than in the past.

With the creation of the State of Israel the Zionist dream had become a reality; yet few Zionists hurried to settle in the promised land. World War II had ended; yet there was no revival of anti-Semitism as the Jews had feared. Every effort to bring a coherent, unified community into being came to nought; yet the Jews were more conscious of their identity at mid-century than they had been for many decades before. These paradoxes revealed that in those same disturbing years after 1920, other broader forces had altered the place of Jews as individuals in American life.

CHAPTER TEN

The Sources of Stability
1920–1954

In a simpler past the Jews had been able to explain themselves as immigrants passing through a melting pot on the way toward being one with other Americans in all but religion. It was thus they had been able to account for their two communities at the opening of the century and for their gradual accommodation to one another and to American society.

After 1920 that view was no longer satisfying. Immigration ceased, but the differences that marked the Jews did not disappear. Instead, rising anti-Semitism revealed the Jews had long been treading in isolation along the edge of a precarious abyss. Furthermore, the end of immigration did not solve the problem of Americanization. Cut off from the ever-replenishing source of culture in Europe, the Jews of the United States were thrown back upon their own resources. Disconnected from Europe and insecure in America, it was essential that they define and explain their situation to themselves.

The old immigrant institutions were fast disappearing. The Yiddish press depended for support upon the continuing stream of new arrivals. Once that was shut off, it entered upon a decline. Its peak came in the mid-1920s when the Yiddish newspapers achieved a daily circulation of some six hundred thousand. By 1940 the total had fallen off by about 50 per cent, and the drop continued thereafter. English pages, first introduced to teach the immigrant to read the language, became bait to draw the interest of younger readers. But the trend was in the other direction. These newspapers had performed their Americanizing task, and were withering away. The Anglo-Jewish weeklies that took their place never attained the same vitality.

The end of immigration also hastened the decline of the Yiddish theater. Young people, strangers to the language, were not interested at all. Many cities gave up their theaters, and were content to rely upon the occasional performances of touring companies. In New York, Maurice Schwartz's Yiddish Art Theater held on, but however valuable in itself, more as a museum piece than as a living force.

The labor movement, once a citadel of Yiddish culture, passed through a troubled period. In the painful decade of the 1920s, in fact until 1933, the membership of the unions had steadily declined from the high point reached during the wartime boom. At the same time, these organizations were wracked by internal struggles stirred up by Communists. All minority groups were fair game to the agitators who hoped to capitalize on the genuine grievances of the workers by holding up the vision of Soviet society—not only classless but free of prejudice. Some Jews responded to the enticing descriptions of the Jewish Republic in Birobidzhan and to the concrete assistance the Party sometimes rendered them. Some also found communist allegiance an outlet for the suppressed pride in Russia, the land of their birth, that they had not theretofore, under the Czars, been able to express. Still others found this the way of showing disappointment with American anti-Semitism. Indefatigably, the communist cells attempted to use this support to capture the unions, whether by boring from within or by setting up dual organizations.

They were not very successful, although they established in some unions, like that of the fur workers, a few hard cores of strength. The old socialist leaders were wary, alerted by the experience of eastern Europe in the decade following the Russian Revolution. The *Daily Forward* was uncompromisingly opposed to the Communists, and the influence of the orthodox elements weighed heavily against the radicals. Only in the middle 1930s and during World War II did the Communists gain a wide audience, and then largely because the Reds temporarily set aside the Party objectives in favor of the policy of the United Front.

Nevertheless, the internal conflict within labor unions in the 1920s was disruptive and confusing. The energies of the leadership were diverted from the main object of improving the workingmen's conditions to that of fighting the Communists within their ranks. Meanwhile some racketeers capitalized on the situation to gain a foothold in a few locals. The membership, confused and disillusioned, drifted into apathy.

The stimulant of the New Deal reinvigorated the labor movement. Communists and racketeers still were active, but both membership and leadership now had clear attainable goals toward which to direct their efforts. The unions in the garment trades regained their strength and entered upon an era of growth that surpassed every earlier achievement. They gave the garment industry enviable stability and their members increasing prosperity. They embarked also upon a program of cultural and social service with many ramifications—in education, the theater, summer camps, and health. But their specifically Jewish character was fading. As the decade advanced, the percentage of Jewish members fell and, although the leadership remained in the old hands, the Amalgamated, the International, and similar unions of necessity became more responsive to the numerous Italians, Puerto Ricans, and Negroes in their ranks. Furthermore, the clothing industries were no longer so heavily concentrated in New York, a fact also reflected in changing union membership. This center of Yiddish culture, that had once embodied the hopes of so many Jewish immigrants, began to be a thing of the past. The arrival of a few thousand refugees from eastern Europe in 1939 and after 1947 did little to restore it.

With immigrant culture on the decline, emphasis shifted to that of the children. Here education was critical. The existing Yiddish and Hebrew schools, shaky at best, showed no capacity for coping with the problem of orienting the rising generation for life as Jews in America. By 1935, in New York, the percentage of children between the ages of six and sixteen who received any Jewish education had dropped to 25 per cent, and seven years later, was still falling. Outside New York the proportion was undoubtedly lower. These measurements may well have been arbitrary. But however one counted up the total, those interested in Jewish education found little ground for complacency. Bureaus of Jewish Education in various cities and a national association attempted to put life into the parochial and part-time school system. But the inescapable questions remained: what were these institutions to teach and why?

Meanwhile the education of Jews, in actuality, remained that offered by the public schools, a vague preparation for the professions which was scarcely capable of readying them for life in their society. Above all, that education was deficient in its comprehension of their particular identity. The implicit premise that every occupant of a seat in the classroom was the same had valuable consequences in a democratic society. But this premise was, in another sense, a drawback in that it deprived the school of the ability to explain to the children it trained the actual differences that divided them.

Consequently, Jews moved often into the wide culture around them without understanding their own relationship to it. They became active participants in the theatrical and literary activities of the nation. Yet their contributions rarely reflected the unique qualities of their antecedents and heritage. Indeed, it sometimes seemed they could achieve success only by divesting themselves of their peculiarities through some gesture at generalization. The creative artists, especially, faced with the problem of satisfying an audience with diffuse, unformulated tastes, attempted to appeal to that audience by shaking off the consciousness of their own different and separate backgrounds. Their work, therefore, betrayed either a self-conscious defensiveness or shunned entirely the problems of their particular experience.

In the early decades of the century, the Yiddish theater had displayed greater vitality than its uptown rivals. Operating within the smaller circle of the group, its writers and actors had been free of the worrisome problem of what the strangers would think and had dealt realistically, yet imaginatively, with the world in which they lived. In that prewar era, the dramas of the Bowery stage had offered a refreshing contrast to the drawing-room farces and melodramas that preempted the boards on Broadway. The Jews active on Broadway had been mostly entrepreneurs. Klaw and Erlanger, Frohman, Belasco, and later the Shuberts had adopted all too readily the assumptions of the uptown world in which they moved. They were organizers and administrators and introduced few changes into the inner content of the American theater.

After 1920, in a more dynamic relationship, the influence of Jews joined a new current of cultural forces that transformed American tastes and pushed the theater in a new direction. The effect of acquaintanceship with the realistic drama of Ibsen, Gorki, Strindberg, and Shaw was probably strongest among Jews who already had such a tradition in the Yiddish past. George Jean Nathan in the field of criticism and the Theater Guild, directed almost entirely by Jews, were the most important agents in the transformation. The Guild provided a stage for the work of Eugene O'Neill and, in its willingness to deal seriously with matters theretofore not known on Broadway, injected a new mood into the theater as a whole.

Yet, significantly, even the Jewish playwrights in these circles did not deal with Jewish themes as such. They thought in terms of universals rather than of particulars. Sidney Kingsley, S. N. Behrman, and George S. Kaufman used character types that were almost anonymous; and Elmer Rice, who handled subjects in which Jews were directly involved, did so in a manner that abstracted and generalized them. *Street Scene,* for instance, set before its audience the recognizable stereotypes of the American city—the studious young Jew, along with the operatic Italian and the fighting Irishman. This play, and Kingsley's *Dead End,* came to grips with the emotional situation of these urban personalities, but it recognized no singularity in its Jewish characters other than their futile resentment of anti-Semitic name-calling.

The tendency toward abstraction in this sense continued through the 1930s and 1940s. Although Jews were now more clearly delineated as persons, they were portrayed most often as types, products of a class or a situation. The theme of the Jew as the victim of an oppressive society was suggested in the writing of Clifford Odets and Arthur Miller. An audience that viewed itself powerless in the grasp of the impersonal forces of depression and war found these dramas moving and evocative of its own position. Anti-Semitism entered these plays tangentially, if at all, yet the dangers of persecution and the sufferings from discrimination added to the insecurities of the authors and similarly affected a large part of the audience.

As the insecurities subsided, the serious drama found itself devoid of themes. The middle-class patrons of the theater, now thriving once more, did not see the same personal threat in McCarthyism that they had once sensed in the demoralizing effects of the depression. Increasingly, their evenings out were devoted to another form of entertainment, which used the same playhouses and enjoyed the prestige of the theater but which had quite different origins and functions.

The musical had its antecedents early in the century in popular vaudeville, a raucous succession of turns that mingled comedy with song, dance with acrobatics, and that drew heavily upon a variety of ethnic stereotypes to attract the masses. The example of European revues and operettas had in the first decades of the twentieth century begun to give tone to these acts. Hung around a loose plot, embellished with a chorus line and lavish sets, these acts were transferred to Broadway in the guise of the musical comedy. Florenz Ziegfeld was active in the transition as a producer, Eddie Cantor, Al Jolson, and Fanny Brice as performers, and Irving Berlin, Jerome Kern, and George Gershwin as composers.

In the 1920s the musicals grew more elaborate and more popular, in keeping with the gaudy atmosphere of the decade. In the process much of their content deteriorated into mere routine. Jews remained prominent, but their work showed no distinctive attributes. In vaudeville, the Jew had been as visible and audible as the Irishman or German or Negro. Now, however, the comedians blurred the outlines of their style to the point at which they were recognizable only by individual peculiarities. The ethnic traits receded and the representative characters, like the Marx Brothers and the Ritz Brothers, were outlandish generalized figures corresponding to nothing that existed off the stage.

For a brief interval in the 1930s this form felt the influence of trends from the contemporary theater. Frivolity lost its charm during the depression, and dwindling audiences demanded more content to these performances. In keeping with the times, the same producers and writers endowed the subject matter with satiric social significance in *Of Thee I Sing*, and *Porgy and Bess*. In such comedies as *Pins and Needles*, created by the ILGWU, and *The Cradle Will Rock* by Mark Blitzstein, there were glimpses of Jewish identities. Nevertheless, even then, the core of the musical revue was the hummable song. After 1939 that became ever more obvious, although an effort was still made to integrate the songs into a story. The typical works of the next decade were the operettas of Rodgers, Hart, and Hammerstein, romantic tales woven skillfully about popular songs that gave the spectators a sense of sensuous and undemanding enjoyment. In this respect their style was drawing closer to that of the movies and, indeed, many of them were written with an eye to ultimate transmigration to Hollywood.

Jews had played a prominent part in every phase of motion-picture production from the very start. But the necessities of a medium that aimed to attract a total audience compelled them to create a product general enough to exert universal appeal. It was only infrequently that a recognizable Jewish character or theme appeared on the screen; and when one did, as in *The Jazz Singer*, it was sentimentalized away from any semblance of reality. Always timid in the face of social issues, the movies, with very rare exceptions, resisted even the challenge of depression in avoiding the troubling problems of American life. After 1941, when the war defined a clear set of acceptable attitudes, there was more evidence of boldness. But generally Hollywood saw its function as entertainment and, toward that end, its techniques depended mostly upon the manipulation of stock figures through stock situations. Within those patterns it made little difference that some of the players, writers, directors, and producers were Jews. Very similar patterns extended to the radio as that medium reached toward a mass audience after 1925.

Only the serious literature of the nation kept open the opportunities for distinctive individual contributions. Unlike the radio or movie, a book could make its way if it found only a few thousand readers; and the smallness of the minimum essential market tolerated differences.

From the end of World War I onward, Jews had occupied important places in such publishing houses as Knopf, Viking, Simon and Shuster, and Random House. In a variety of ways, they had influenced the book trade. They were, in part at least, responsible for introducing the works of contemporary Continental authors to the United States, for uncovering new writers, and for developing cheap forms of book production for wide circulation.

While the medium allowed more individuality than the radio or theater, the writers were nonetheless subject to the dilemmas of their own identification in American society. The most popular Jewish authors were those like Fannie Hurst or Edna Ferber who wrote, in the common magazine style of the 1920s, sentimental stories usually set in rural or small-town America, stories which celebrated the simple virtues and confirmed the accepted values of their readers. These tales, for all their craftsmanlike composition, had little substance; their superficial homilies were only slightly relevant to the meaningful problems of the day. They had no relationship at all to the circumstances of American Jews.

On the other hand, from Abraham Cahan's *Rise of David Levinsky* to Daniel Fuchs's *Low Company*, a line of novels described the life of the Jews in harsh naturalistic terms. These works had the virtue of verisimilitude. Often they contained valuable observations and insights. But often the authors also treated their subjects as if all human qualities were simply overwhelmed by the misery and filth of the environment.

The depression heightened the attractiveness of these novels by emphasizing the significance of the social commentary in them. Tess Slesinger, Michael Gold, Jerome Weidman, Albert Halper, Meyer Levin, and a number of others created the image of the Jew as a total victim of the exploitive order under which they lived. Like James T. Farrell and Richard Wright, who treated other ethnic groups, the burden of their theme was that the Jew, or Irishman, or Negro was different only in so far as the slum debased him. Toward the end of the 1930s the source of oppression was more often anti-Semitism and less often capitalism. Irwin Shaw and Arthur Miller were among the young writers who reacted violently to the threat of anti-Semitism at home, of Nazism abroad, and of impending war. Their works were full of the figures of violence, in a genre that would later lead to the war novels of Norman Mailer and Herman Wouk. These stories too portrayed the Jew primarily as a victim—one who, though he retaliated, still was selected for his role by external circumstances rather than by any positive identification from within his own personality.

The qualities Jews brought to American culture originated in their situation in American society. On the one hand, as producers, publishers, and impresarios, they were innovating enterprisers. As outsiders, they were to some degree less bound by habit and convention than those more comfortably relaxed in the customs of the country. As members of a group with a distinctive cultural heritage that reached back to Europe, the Jews were able to make fertile comparisons and contrasts. Finally, as newcomers, they were compelled to take risks with the untried because that often was the only means of breaking into the ranks of those already established. The Jews, therefore, were a fresh current, stimulating and quickening the main stream of American culture.

They played a similar part in helping to introduce modern art and modern music to the United States. Earlier in the century, a few Jews of wealth had pursued the interests common to their peers. Benjamin Altman had collected renaissance paintings and Otto Kahn and Oscar Hammerstein had been patrons of the opera. But more often, even the Jews who earned fortunes were not able to compete with the Morgans and Fricks for old masters or for boxes in the diamond horseshoe. The possession of such symbols of status was not as valuable to people who did not in any case aspire to acceptance in high society, and who were alien to the religious symbolism in the Mass or the cathedral.

Instead, Jews found attractive a style of art sensitive to difference; they looked ahead toward the new rather than back to the traditional. The tendency toward abstraction in Continental painting and music now evoked a particularly vivid response in those Jews who had moved away from their own tradition and were unwilling to adopt any other. The Guggenheims and Edgar Kaufmann, Minna Lederman and Alma Morgenthau, among others, sponsored the works of contemporary Europeans and of Americans influenced by them. In the arts, prejudice was irrelevant and talent and taste alone counted.

The acknowledged contributions of prominent Jews to all walks of American life increased the security and stimulated the pride of American Jews at large. Hank Greenberg was accepted as an outstanding baseball player as Macy's was accepted as a popular department store. Artur Rubenstein played the piano, Bernard Baruch advised presidents, and Adolph S. Ochs published the finest newspaper in the land. Their achievements were admired by everyone; in this sense their leadership in so many diverse fields acted as a powerful factor in helping to integrate their fellow Jews into American life.

There was little, however, that was distinctively Jewish in the achievements of the men and women who attained fame in the 1920s and 1930s. By and large they followed the trends already established in the theater, in the mass entertainment industries, and in literature. Such conformity imparted a quality of inauthenticity to their work. Rarely did their work deal with the experiences that were closest to them. The occasional Jewish figures who appeared in their creations were generalized as if they were exactly like all other people, or else, if they were different, had been made so by such disastrous external forces as the depression or anti-Semitism.

The Jews in the audience took pride in the success of the men of letters and actors who had gained the recognition of the widest American society. As part of the audience the Jews enjoyed the blackfaced antics of comedians and their interest was held by novels like *So Big*. But they could not establish the rapport their parents in the Bowery gallery had felt for the characters of *God, Man, and the Devil*. For the problems of deepest significance in their lives were not explored by the intellectuals and artists they respected.

To the extent that this void persisted, the problem of Jewish identification was left in the hands of a few philosophers and theorists within the community. But their concepts commanded no wide support. Their ideas, phrased in terms of a

self-enclosed community, seemed far removed from the ac-
tualities of American life. The mass of Jews who were both
Americans and Jews worked out the problems of their accommodation pragmatically and without direction.

The most attractive effort to contrive a philosophy of Jewish life in terms of American experience still looked back to its
antecedents in immigration. Back in 1915 Horace M. Kallen
had incisively questioned the melting-pot theory. Already he
perceived that life in the United States did not totally dissolve
group differences, and he suggested instead that the freedom
and complexity of this society not only tolerated but encouraged diversities. He thought of the United States as a great
orchestra in which the instruments retained their individual
voices and played not in unison but in harmony, adding rich-
ness to the whole by their very distinctiveness. This image of
cultural pluralism was highly compelling through the 1920s
and 1930s. It supplied reassurance to many who sought a firm
basis for belonging to both Judaism and America.

Cultural pluralism also supplied the ideological foundation for the reconstructionist movement. Dr. Mordecai M.
Kaplan came increasingly to view Judaism as a changing civilization. The reconstructionist saw a quality of dynamic unity
in the group, a unity that expressed itself in common identification, common language, literature, music, and folkways.
From this point of view, it made sense to preserve traditional
customs and ceremonies without inquiring into their theological meaning. By stimulating nostalgic memories, reconstructionists hoped to find a way of holding the group together;
yet by not insisting on punctilious religious conformity, they

tried to allow the Jews, in contacts outside the group, to act as other Americans.

The ideas of the reconstructionists supplied a fresh reason for being to the YMHAs and similar institutions. The National Jewish Welfare Board, at first a wartime agency to serve the men in the Armed Forces, after 1918 had found a function in coordinating and guiding the diverse Y's and neighborhood houses. These community centers, however, now shifted their emphasis from the task of Americanizing the immigrant Jews to imparting Jewish culture to the native Americans. The end of immigration had resolved the old problems and the search for identification had created new ones. To Dr. Kaplan the center was the logical unit of community organization, and his disciples labored to make these agencies over in accordance with his ideas. The adoption of the recommendations of the Janowsky Survey in 1948 formally committed the Welfare Board to the proposition that the programs of the Jewish center should stress "Jewish content." Since "Jewish content" was never clearly defined, however, that action expressed little more than the hope that little Jewish islands would survive in the great sea of Americanism.

Neither cultural pluralism nor the philosophy of the reconstructionists drew much support from the dominant intellectual currents of the three decades after World War I. In the 1920s these formulas ran into headlong conflict with nationalism of two kinds. The 100-per-center, whether ardently Jewish or violently American, did not admit any such pluralistic view of culture, but insisted upon defining it in terms of some total and unchanging allegiance. For these two extremes—those distressed by foreign-sounding names and those who insisted that every aspect of communal life be parochially Jewish—there was little room for a middle ground.

Often the generation that matured after 1920 found it tempting to try to become entirely American without any vestige of Judaism, or entirely Jewish detached from the America in which they lived. Some dropped their Jewish affiliations entirely and drifted into the anonymous mass of city dwellers without formal institutional connections of any sort. They were reluctant to seem to be either yielding to or escaping from anti-Semitism. Now and then a gnawing question arose as to whether this was not, after all, simply the easiest way out, a subtle type of cowardice, while others suffered or were threatened with suffering. But such qualms could be stilled by immersing in a vague general liberalism or by embracing one of the radicalisms that promised, among other results, to bring about the extinction of anti-Semitism and the abolition of all group differences.

Or, conversely, a relatively few Jews after 1920 turned inward to their own group more intensely. Their present life was tolerable, on whatever level, because they were only sojourners in the United States and expected at some remote date to be off in a new exodus to the promised land. Every slight and insult, every act of hostility was expected, almost welcomed, as confirmatory evidence that they were right in not belonging. Their eyes on Zion, zeal served them as a protective shield against the bruising encounters with a world of which they wished no part.

Neither extreme attracted the mass of Jews who remained what they were, Jews in America, at home there and in their own way contriving a style of life out of the practical necessities about them. They acted as the specific demands of each occasion seemed to require, without regard to ideological implications. If they supported the New Deal, it was not out of faith in the abstract doctrines of liberalism but out of the desire for relief from depression and discrimination. If they supported Jewish settlement in Palestine, it was not out of adherence to the nationalistic ideas of the Zionist theorists but out of their own insecurity and out of the sense of obligations to the victims of Nazism. Neither route of escape offered the great majority of the American Jews any adequate explanation of the process in which they were actually involved.

In any case, those divergent roads led only into dead ends. The spread of Hitlerism, the desolation of the war, and the betrayal by the Soviet Union of the old socialist ideals made it increasingly difficult for the unaffiliated to remain aloof, to hope that the problem of their own identification would ultimately be dissolved in some magic disappearance of the Jewish problem. What was more, as they married and established families they discovered that America was not, after all, a land of unaffiliated men. The children's questions could not be answered if everyone else did somehow belong.

As for Zionism as an ideology, that escape vanished with the establishment of Israel. The few who imagined they would themselves migrate to the promised land and the larger number who expected that from it would emanate the influences to redeem the life of the Jews in exile were alike disappointed. When the long-awaited day finally came, there was no exodus. In vain persuasive voices urged the confirmed Zionists to migrate. They would not go. With the way open, they discovered at once that it was not on that far Mediterranean shore they belonged, but where they were in America.

Moreover, it was idle to think Israel could immediately play a redeeming role. The realities of the new state scarcely promised soon to bring alive the hopes attached to it. Intermittent war and prolonged financial stringency made it unlikely that impulses from Israel would mitigate anti-Semitism or generate the cultural, social, and economic renaissance the Zionists in exile had anticipated. As that awareness dawned, the most zealous knew their dreams had been but dreams to hide the knowledge of the day. There was no alternative now but to seek the meaning of their lives in the United States, for they would remain permanently a part of American society.

In the 1940s many errant spirits sought in weariness the peace of faith. The theology of crisis offered some Protestants who sought it a mode of conversion that was intellectually respectable. The adherents of Catholicism dropped the apologetic tone of their writings in earlier decades. In the face of developing events, who could deny the evil in man or the overriding necessity for tradition, faith, and authority?

For a few Jews, too, the secular gods had failed, and only a return to the ancestral Deity remained. If ever doubts stirred—whether it was now possible to recapture the belief in an immanent God directly observing every human act and transgression—such doubts were thoroughly stifled. Sinking back into the pillowed round of ritual, the disillusioned, puffed up new illusions, created a romantic vision of the old ghetto, a secure and self-contained place of piety and good deeds, and longed to be taken back.

The past century and a half, they asserted, had been an error based upon "ugly and transitory fallacies." The "so-called emancipation" was now crumbling into dust. Only the "crippled Jews," the adherents "of servile assimilationism" still blindly accepted it. Its symbols in America were "baseball, gin rummy, the average Hollywood film, and the comic strip."

But there was a troublesome stumbling block! To what religion should they return? By now the Jews of the United States had left far behind the orthodoxy of their grandparents and had moved well along the way to precisely such an accommodation to American culture as the seekers after faith despised. For those to whom religion was a part of life and not an escape from it, the practices of synagogue and home were integrated with the manners of the society in which they lived—with television and democracy and not with the study hall of the ghetto.

Perhaps there was a touch of comic incongruity to Uncle Max the Chanukah Man who brought his pack of gifts on the holiday and told the children edifying stories. But there was also in the notion an element of courageous effort to bring the religious heritage of the past into some direct relationship with a day-to-day existence in the present that was not limited by the horizons of the *shtetl*.

In any case, the Judaism of American Jews did not remain an accumulation of inviolately guarded souvenirs but rather, exposed to the open influences of the milieu, changed in response to the needs of its adherents. The orthodox *shul* took on some of the appearances of the temple and in countless details traditional practice was transformed. The conservative congregations had long been receptive to innovations which proceeded rapidly and almost without their awareness. By contrast, a "neo-reform" trend had introduced some of the accents of orthodoxy into the reform movement and had pulled it back from its advanced position of the nineteenth century.

The whole process of religious redefinition had its roots in American soil. It was not theory or theological speculation that led the Jews in the United States more often than formerly to order their communal life around religion, but rather the terms of the society in which they lived. As their immigrant antecedents receded, their identification remained most meaningful in the area of diversity which America most clearly recognized, that of religion.

And religion in that sense meant the pattern of activities that drew the group together and located it in the universe, that drew its children onward and cemented family relationships. It was indeed the Brotherhood and Sisterhood, the adult-education lecture and benefit card party, the temple dance where boy met girl, and the familiar conviviality of the supper club. The participants in the "Purim barn dance" swung their partners without worrying whether it was the "Jewish content" or the "American environment" that moved them. As the recollection of the dangerous obligations of the quarter-century after World War I receded, Americans turned increasingly to the temple and the synagogue for what they found there: peace of mind in the company of their fellows and emotional satisfaction for the whole personality.

Not many were conscious of the deeper, less perceptible changes that lay beyond the alterations in communal and religious life. Beneath the surface shifts in organizations and policies lay a massive reordering of all the elements in the group's composition. The ultimate effects were still to be felt in the future.

The consequences of the end of immigration steadily made themselves apparent after 1925. The restrictive quota laws shut the United States off as a refuge for those who might otherwise have fled, after 1933, from the persecutions of the Nazis in Germany and of other reactionary governments in Poland, Hungary, and Romania. As it was, only a few got through, perhaps 170,000 in all, between Hitler's accession to power and the end of the second war. The refugee program after 1947 added scarcely 100,000 more, not enough to influence the existing communities substantially.

One result of the slackening of immigration had been a natural transfer of the control of all communal activities in time to the native-born. A further result was the retardation of the rate of growth of the Jewish population. By the outbreak of World War II, the number of Jews in the United States had been stabilized at between four and a half and five million, and there it remained. There was thereafter some shifting about of population as a few communities gained while others lost, but the total stayed about the same.

While the end of immigration prevented accretions from abroad, other indigenous factors were also operating to level off the rate of population growth. The average age of the group was rising, and its family size was falling to below the national average. Proportionately, there were more older and fewer younger people in the group.

After 1920 the economic and social extremes among the Jews tended to become less marked. Furthermore, the charac-

teristics of Jewish businesses were changing. The great banking houses were less dependent upon European capital and
connections than before World War I. The old Jewish firms
gradually lost their family character and acquired boards of
directors almost indistinguishable from those of other American banks. The number of Jews active in finance did not grow.

On the other hand, in the decades after the enactment of
the quota laws, the Jewish working class all but disappeared.
It had earlier existed only in the largest cities; elsewhere the
Jews were absorbed in trade and in clerical occupations. Now
the number of those who worked for wages declined steadily,
even in New York. The old hands were dying off, their sons
did not take their places, and no new Jewish laborers appeared.
In 1950 such workers were distinctly a minority in many
branches of the garment industries into which so many Jewish tears and hopes were sewn.

Nor was there a corresponding increase in the number of
shopkeepers and petty tradesmen. The trend toward large-
scale enterprise, toward department and chain stores, made the
process of beginning at the bottom less attractive to the native
young men who, in any case, were not inclined toward the
backbreaking toil and the self-denial of their parents. These
people were more likely to move into the professions and into
salaried employments. It was not the Nobel prize winners,
I. I. Rabi or S. A. Waksman or the internationally famous
physicists, Albert Einstein and Robert Oppenheimer, who
were distinctive of this period; such men would have made
their mark in any time and place. But it was a new departure
to find scores of Jews of average ability at work in laboratories
and offices on the same terms as their fellow citizens. The

expansion of those ranks, particularly after 1939, showed both the extent to which discriminatory practices had subsided and the changing character of the group's ambitions.

Jews fell in also with the general drift of population toward the Pacific Coast and some parts of the South. In the 1920s they had become involved in the booms in Florida and in California, and they continued to move in those directions in the next two decades. By mid-century there were more than 300,000 in Los Angeles and more than 50,000 in Miami. The shift was in part due to the attractions of a warm climate for a group growing more elderly and more prosperous. In part it was due to the general migration of industry away from the Northeast, a migration that now took other Jews to the hills of Tennessee and North Carolina and the plains of the Gulf states. Finally, soldiers, who had been trained in remote parts of the country, were tempted after the war to leave the old cities for the opportunities of the new places. Soon after there were Jewish communities in every state of the union.

One way or another, the Jews were coming to conform to the standards of middle-class life in America. Having acquired respectable employment, they moved off in ever larger numbers to discover respectable housing in the suburbs. On the periphery of the great cities they built comfortable homes and adopted the appropriate symbols of their status. The size of their families shrank as did that of other Americans at this social level.

Middle-class necessities and ideals increasingly permeated communal life. There were fewer calls upon the welfare agencies for relief of pauperism and more frequent calls for advice on the relief of personality maladjustments. The children were sent off to better schools, but were cautioned not to study too hard and instructed to have a good time. When Brandeis University was established in the 1940s, it was a nonsectarian institution, away from the city, in the rural setting and with the curriculum of the conventional American college. The boys and girls, whether at Brandeis or at any other school, ceased to be the bookish lot of the 1920s and were as likely to let their thoughts run ahead to careers in business as to those in the professions. Meanwhile, their parents laid out a new synagogue as well as a country club and a modern hospital, and were active in the PTAs of the public and the Sunday school, in the Red Cross and Hadassah, in Rotary and B'nai B'rith.

Once, the intrusion of Jews into a new neighborhood had been resented, and restrictive covenants had been adopted to prevent their coming. Occasionally such gentlemen's agreements were still effective, but ever more frequently they became anachronistic. In many but not all of the new residential areas, the Jews who came at the same time clustered in fairly homogeneous blocks. But outsiders found it pointless after a while to notice the appearance of the newcomers who, on closer inspection, proved no different from other new neighbors. The old stereotype of the mysterious Jew had largely disappeared, wiped out by the middle-class respectability of his descendants.

The evolving style of life of the group fell imperceptibly into the molds of American middle-class culture, although retaining distinctive features derived from the past. In homes, indistinguishable in appearance from those on any other street, the Jews now soaked up the tastes and values of *Life* and *The*

New Yorker and the Book-of-the-Month Club. They lived in a world given form by the images of movies and television, and found themselves increasingly at home there. They moved into the crowd of eager spectators, absorbed in athletic contests, not merely—as formerly—partisans of an occasional Benny Leonard or Maxie Baer, but like other Americans, committed rooters for a team. The Jews retained a sentimental attachment to Israel, took pride in the achievements of the new state, and added it to the itinerary of their European tour. They were themselves none the less American. The ladies gathered for Hadassah's tea stepped out of the pages of *Vogue*. Even the arrangement of the synagogue, the traditional appurtenances of worship, and the religious ceremonies showed the effects of change wrought by the American environment.

The environment of the 1940s encouraged the adjustment. The war and the consolidated gains of the New Deal had stifled anti-Semitism along with the exclusive isolationism from which it sprang. The old restrictive nationalism was still capable of rising up as it did in 1952 in the McCarran-Walter Act. But there was no longer any overt challenge to the place of the Jews and other ethnic groups in American life.

As the problems of being both Jewish and American grew less imposing, there was a relaxation of tension in the face of the whole society. Consequently, the Jews demanded less and got more from their participation in American culture. As they became more and more assimilated to middle-class tastes, special explanations of their own situation as a group were not so necessary. At the same time, as they were increasingly more accepted as figures on the American scene, they appeared naturally for what they were in the drama, the movies, and on the radio. A comedy like *The Fifth Season* and movies like *Gentlemen's Agreement* dealt with their position as Jews in human, realistic terms, for all the world to see. A few of the comics on radio and television dropped the effort at ethnic anonymity. Writers like Delmore Schwartz and Isaac Rosenfeld described without self-consciousness the experience of being a Jew, just as now Ralph Ellison and James Baldwin dealt with the Negro as a person rather than as a problem.

The process was to some extent reciprocal, since American culture was itself fluid and responsive to the presence of many diverse groups, including the Jews. Thus in the movies of John Garfield, in the television antics of Milton Berle, in the novels of Saul Bellow, and in the language of the comic strips, a much wider audience began to catch glimpses of what Jews were.

Sometimes, perhaps, the Jews wondered whether something valuable was not lost in the accommodation. Now that few remnants of the immigrant culture remained, the idealized image of the ghetto was strangely fascinating, in its implacable resistance to change, in its stubborn devotion to learning. But the ghetto was gone, and only in idle daydreams, which blotted out reality, was there any inclination to restore it. More often Jews took pride in what had persisted. The strength of family life had not been seriously shaken. Indications were that the divorce rate was substantially below the national average and that the relationship of Jewish parents and children remained intimate and cohesive.

The sense that philanthropy was a binding ethical obligation survived also. The funds raised for overseas relief had passed their peak in 1948 when $150,000,000 had been collected, but the decline thereafter was more a reflection of diminished needs than of shirked responsibilities. Donations for domestic institutions did not appreciably fall off, nor did Jews fail to remain aware of their responsibilities toward more general communal causes.

Finally, nothing that had happened since 1939 dimmed the consciousness of Jews of their obligations as a group to continue to fight for the rights of free men in a free society. That their own grievances had largely been satisfied did not diminish the obligation to continue the struggle on behalf of the still underprivileged groups.

The McCarran-Walter Act of 1952 was a striking illustration. Coming when there were no longer any substantial numbers of Jews seeking to migrate to the United States, the measure did not directly affect American Jews as a group. Yet they took the lead in opposing the Act. They did so instinctively because its monstrous racist provisions grossly contravened the ideals of justice and human equality they had come as Americans to value.

Even the comfortably middle class deeply resented discriminations practiced not against themselves or their co-religionists but against unknown Poles and Greeks and Italians. It was not in the least self-interest that moved them; rather it was the recollection that they or their parents, like other Americans, had all once been strangers, looking toward this land for freedom. In this response, as in their earlier and continued activity on behalf of the Negro in such organizations as the National Association for the Advancement of Colored People, they showed they still aligned themselves on the side of those whose rights were sometimes denied. Their continued involve-

ment in the battles for other men's liberties was nourished by
the awareness that in America there was no group that was not
by some reckoned a minority, and that all must be zealous in
defense of their individual freedom.

Perhaps these were the most valuable elements of the rich
heritage they carried on into the future.

Looking backward from 1954, the three hundred years of
Jewish life in the United States seem an adventure in freedom.
Wandering, at first almost by accident and then in a great
mass movement, the Jews had moved into a society unlike any
they had encountered in their previous existence. Of that society they became at once a part. With it they experienced,
in turn, the pressures of growth, the liberation from European
political dominance, the exhilaration of conquering a continent, and the difficult responsibilities of leadership in a
troubled and disordered world. For a long interval—almost a
half-century—their place was questioned by bitter, fearful
men, until reassertion of a more tolerant tradition reestablished
their security and stability.

In the course of this history, the adjustments the Jews made
were novel and often trying. But they had a large meaning
for themselves and for mankind. Their children, now fully
American, have no firsthand knowledge of the Old World or
of the difficulties of the transition from it. But they can learn
from that experience the values inherent in the institutions
that still surround them.

Migration drew together from every part of Europe Jews
long separated. They learned, though painfully, to live together
in the United States while respecting each other's differences.

From time to time Sephardim questioned the desirability of the Ashkenazim, Germans of east Europeans, and Lithuanians of Galicians. But no effort to impose uniformity upon the group as a whole achieved the least degree of success. Rather, these diversities permitted various groups to pursue their own ways and proved creative, in the interests of all. American society as a whole in these years also learned the perils of a stultifying homogeneity and the potentialities of diversity.

In their recent past in Europe the Jews had lived in established Jewish communities, recognized and regulated by law, and endowed with power over the lives of their members. In the New World the law took no cognizance of their character as a group. The community had no means of compulsion over its members, who could withdraw if they wished and who, if they continued to adhere to it, did so of their own free will. Financial support for Jewish activities could not come by taxation, nor discipline by fear. Instead modes of governing by consent developed slowly but consistently. More effectively than by taxation, the Jews of the United States raised funds by philanthropic giving, and more effectively than by coercion, they regulated themselves by accord.

In the ordered society of Europe the Jews had accepted a closed system of status with a hierarchy of superior and inferior ranks. They recognized differences in rights and obligations between themselves and other elements in society. And within their own group they took for granted the existence of well-nigh impassable barriers between the learned, the wealthy, the toilers. In America, after the eighteenth century, the law was ever less likely to recognize such gradations of rank. After the Revolution all men stood equal in the eyes of the state. Within the group, as within the whole society, they were one in rights and obligations.

In the Old World the Jews had lived hemmed in by innumerable restrictions. From without, they were crowded into the ghetto and limited to a narrow round of life, economically, socially, and politically. From within, they bore the burden of a tradition narrowly and rigidly construed and controlled by a small group of individuals who dominated the mass.

The Atlantic crossing was liberating. In every area of life the confining regulations fell away and man was left free, within the rules general to all, to pursue his trade and calling, to act as man and citizen without interference from the state.

Freedom entailed responsibilities both as to the ends and the means of social action. The general welfare was the goal of men's communal and political life; in all matters binding on the whole, decisions were the will of the majority, which nevertheless respected the rights of the minority. In this spirit, democracy became a way of life that reordered the Jewish communities.

Diversity, voluntarism, equality, freedom, and democracy—these were the products of three centuries of experience in America. In their attainment, the Jews shattered the closed ghettoes of the Old World and replaced them with voluntary communities of free men, governing themselves in accord with their own interests. The apparent chaos of the eighteenth and early nineteenth centuries gradually yielded to a general pattern of free communal action. The diverse strains of immigration in the hundred years after 1825 prevented the society from settling immediately into any fixed mold and enriched its experience with new elements. In the more recent period of greater stability and maturity, successive crises have tried the old values, which have not been found wanting. And, though nothing remains free of change, the Jews of America await a future in which they expect still to find the projections of their adventure of the past.

Suggestions for Further Reading

The note that follows describes the most important available works in English that may be consulted by readers interested in pursuing the subject further.

There is no good complete general history of the Jews in the United States. Lee J. Levinger, *History of the Jews in the United States* (1935) is rather old-fashioned, as are Peter Wiernick, *History of the Jews in America* (1912) and Isaac Markens, *Hebrews in America* (1888). Anita L. Lebeson, *Pilgrim People* (1950) is anecdotal and disorganized. Less pretentious, but perhaps more rewarding, are the volumes of little essays by Lee M. Friedman, *Jewish Pioneers and Patriots* (1942) and *Pilgrims in a New Land* (1948). Occasional articles in a number of periodicals are more enlightening. The most valuable publications include: *American Jewish Historical Society Publications* (annual and quarterly; 1892–date); *American Jewish Year Book* (annual; 1899–date); *Commentary* (monthly; 1945–date); *American Jewish Archives* (semi-annual; 1948–date); and *Yivo Annual of Jewish Social Science* (1946–date).

The *American Jewish Historical Society Publications* also frequently include transcriptions of documents. Morris U. Schappes, *Documentary History of the Jews in the United States, 1654–1875* (1950) is a useful collection although marred by the Marxist bias of its author. Moses Rischin, *Inventory of American Jewish History* (1954) is a convenient guide to all such material.

The history of the Jews in the colonial period has been most thoroughly examined. Jacob R. Marcus, *Early American Jewry* (2 vols., 1951–1952) has replaced all earlier studies. It deals with the whole range of Jewish life in the seventeenth and eighteenth centuries. It may be supplemented by some of the local studies mentioned below and by A. V. Goodman, *American Overture* (1947).

The experience of the first three quarters of the nineteenth century has been most seriously neglected. Apart from a few local and biographical studies, the most useful contributions have been those of Rudolf Glanz, *Jews in Relation to the Cultural Media of the Germans in America* (1947) and Guido Kisch, *In Search of Freedom, a History of American Jews from Czechoslovakia* (1949). Both deal with restricted subjects, however. B. W. Korn's *American Jewry and the Civil War* (1951) includes the results of painstaking research.

The east European migration has been better handled, although a good deal of the best work is in Yiddish, not accessible to the readers of English. Charles S. Bernheimer, *Russian Jew in the United States* (1905) is a contemporary work with a good deal of information. Hutchins Hapgood, *Spirit of the Ghetto* (1902) is a study by a sympathetic reporter. Samuel Joseph, *Jewish Immigration to the United States* (1914) is largely a statistical study.

The last groups of immigrants, the refugees, have been treated in Maurice R. Davie, *Refugees in America* (1947) and by Donald P. Kent, *The Refugee Intellectual* (1953).

A number of biographies and autobiographies supply revealing insight into the life of American Jews. Cyrus Adler, *I Have Considered the Days* (1941) and his *Jacob H. Schiff* (2 vols., 1928) deal with important communal leaders. Isaac M. Wise,

Reminiscences (1901); David Philipson, *My Life as an American Jew* (1937); and Stephen S. Wise, *Challenging Years* (1949), are accounts by American rabbis. Mary Antin, *The Promised Land* (1917) is the story of an immigrant. M. U. Blaustein, *Memoirs of David Blaustein* (1913); Boris D. Bogen, *Born a Jew* (1938); and Philip Cowen, *Memories of an American Jew* (1932), give the story of men active in communal life. Marvin Lowenthal, *Henrietta Szold* (1942) throws light on early American Zionism. Gustav Pollak, *Michael Heilprin and His Sons* (1912) deals with the middle nineteenth century. Oscar S. Strauss, *Under Four Administrations* (1922); Henry Morgenthau, *All in a Life-time* (1922); A. T. Mason, *Brandeis* (1946); and Joseph M. Proskauer, *A Segment of My Times* (1950), deal with figures active in politics. Lillian D. Wald, *House on Henry Street* (1915) and *Windows on Henry Street* (1934); and Jane Addams, *Twenty Years at Hull House* (1910) are the memoirs of social workers. There are numerous biographies of the theatrical figures mentioned in the text.

Local communal studies cover a wide range. Hyman B. Grinstein, *Rise of the Jewish Community of New York* (1945) deals with the period from 1654 to 1860. Additional information is in Robert Ernst, *Immigrant Life in New York City* (1949). Charles Reznikoff, *Jews of Charleston* (1950) treats the most important early Southern community but may be supplemented by B. A. Elzas, *Jews of South Carolina* (1905). P. P. Bregstone, *Chicago and Its Jews* (1933); Hull House, *Maps and Papers* (1895); H. L. Meites, *History of the Jews of Chicago* (1924); Louis Wirth, *The Ghetto* (1928); and M. A. Gutstein, *Priceless Heritage* (1953), deal with the second American city. H. E. Ezekiel and Gaston Lichtenstein, *History of the Jews of Richmond* (1917); Henry S. Morais, *Jews of Philadelphia* (1894); Joshua Trachtenberg, *Con-*

sider the Years (1944); and R. A. Woods, *City Wilderness* (1898), handle other American cities.

The Jewish labor movement has been the subject of several special studies; the most important, that conducted by Yivo, however, is incomplete. The following works are useful: Melech Epstein, *Jewish Labor in the U.S.A.* (2 vols., 1950–1953); Wilfred Carsel, *History of the Chicago Ladies' Garment Workers Union* (1940); John R. Commons, et al., *History of Labor in the United States* (4 vols., 1935–1936); R. W. DeForest and Lawrence Veiller, *Tenement House Problem* (2 vols., 1903); Herbert Harris, *American Labor* (1938); I. A. Hourwich, *Immigration and Labor* (1912); and Benjamin Stolberg, *Tailor's Progress* (1944).

Works on other special subjects include Sophia M. Robison, *Jewish Population Studies* (1943); Ben M. Edidin, *Jewish Community Life in America* (1947); Boris D. Bogen, *Jewish Philanthropy* (1917); Gabriel Davidson, *Our Jewish Farmers* (1943); David Philipson, *Reform Movement in Judaism* (1941); Cyrus Adler, *Jewish Theological Seminary* (1939). Albert I. Gordon, *Jews in Transition* (1949) is the most successful effort to analyze the contemporary situation.

Among the useful works on the European background are Salo W. Baron, *Social and Religious History of the Jews* (3 vols., 1937), a revision of which is in progress, and the same author's *Jewish Community* (3 vols., 1940). Shorter surveys of Jewish history include A. L. Sachar, *History of the Jews* (1953), and Solomon Grayzel, *Short History* (1904). On the Jews of eastern Europe, S. N. Dubnow, *History of the Jews in Russia and Poland* (3 vols., 1912–1915) is useful. Mark Wischnitzer, *To Dwell in Safety* (1948) is the best account of Jewish emigration from Europe.

Glossary

Am Olam: a movement of Russian intellectuals in the 1880s, seeking a return to agriculture in America and in Palestine.

Ashkenaz: Germany. — *Ashkenazim:* Germans or, more loosely, Jews, including those of eastern Europe who followed the German ritual.

Baal Shem Tov: Known by the initials as Besht. Chasidic mystic, 1700–1760.

Bar Mitzvah: ceremony at which boys at the age of thirteen assume the religious duties of adults.

Bayerische: Bavarian.

Besht: see Baal Shem Tov.

Beth Din: Religious court of justice.

Bikur Cholim: society for visiting and aiding the sick.

Bilu: group of Russian Jewish students who emigrated to Palestine in 1880s.

Chasidism: eighteenth-century mystical sect.

Cheder: religious elementary school.

Chevra: congregation or association.

Daitchuk: German.

Gemilath Chasodim: loan society.

Get: divorce; also the document that creates the divorce.

Haskalah: enlightenment movement in the last quarter of the eighteenth century.

Hazan: cantor. — *Hazanim:* cantors.

Hinter-Berliner: from beyond Berlin; Jews from eastern Germany.

Kaddish: memorial service recited by sons in the first year of their parents' death, and on fixed occasions thereafter.

Kahal: Congregation.

Kashruth: ritual laws of behavior, particularly dietary.

Kehillah: community organization (— *oth*, plural).

Landsman: countryman; emigrant from the same town.

Landsmannschaften: organizations of countrymen.

Lishmo: for its own sake.

Maschgiach: functionary who supervises the adherence to ritual in the preparation of foods and certifies their *kashruth*.

Maskilim: the enlightened; particularly participants in the Haskalah movement.

Melamed: teacher.

Minyan: the ten men who constitute a congregation.

Mitzvo: a ritual commandment.

Mohel: circumciser (— *im*, plural).

Nogid: man of wealth.

Nusach: order of religious services.

Pak Tsores: bag of woes.

Pogrom: riot against Jews. — *Pogromchik:* participant in such a riot.

Pushke: collection box for charity.

Rebbe: teacher.

Schnorrer: beggar.

Sephardim: Spanish; those who follow the ritual common in southern Europe.

Shaitel: wig.

Shamas: beadle.

Shohet: ritual slaughterer.

Shul: synagogue.

Shtadlan: influential Jew in a position to intercede for his coreligionists.

Stetl: east European Jewish village.

Tachlis: purpose.

Talmud Torah: part-time Hebrew school.

Torah: Pentateuch; also the whole body of traditional learning derived from it.

Tsore: affliction; metaphorically, wife.

Yeshiva: institution of higher religious learning.

Yom Kippur: Day of Atonement. — *Yom Kippur Ball:* radical festivities in deliberate violation of orthodox regulations for observance of the holiday.

Zaddik: holy man; one who observes all the commandments; also a mystic saint, or leader of a chasidic group.

Index

271